Child's Play
Quick and Easy Costumes

Also by Leslie Hamilton

Child's Play: 200 Instant Crafts and Activities for Preschoolers

Child's Play 6–12

Child's Play Quick and Easy Costumes

Written and illustrated by
Leslie Hamilton

Crown Trade Paperbacks
New York

Published by Crown Trade Paperbacks, 201 East 50th Street, New York, New York 10022. Member of the Crown Publishing Group.

Random House, Inc. New York, Toronto, London, Sydney, Auckland

Crown Trade Paperbacks and colophon are trademarks of Crown Publishers, Inc.

Manufactured in the United States of America

LIBRARY OF CONGRESS CATALOGING-IN-PUBLICATION DATA

Hamilton, Leslie, 1950–
Child's Play: quick and easy costumes / Leslie Hamilton.—1st ed.
p.   cm.
Includes index.
1. Children's clothing.   2. Costume.   3. Children—Costume.
I. Title
TT635.H34   1995
646.4'78—dc20
94-33148
CIP

ISBN 0-517-88173-X

10 9 8 7 6 5 4 3 2 1

First Edition

To my mom
Judith Pearlman
with love and gratitude.

CONTENTS

ACKNOWLEDGMENTS

Beryl Anderson and Vivian Pearlman took time from their busy schedules to critique my manuscript, offering invaluable suggestions, insights, and advice. Their comments and cross-country conversations are deeply appreciated.

Thanks also to Dave Hamilton, Sarah Hamilton, Robert Pearlman, Lynn Howard, Mo Guy, and Jennifer Galloway for sharing their costume ideas with me.

Special thanks and love to my husband, Larry, for his suggestions, encouragement, and computer help.

Cressida Connolly and Kim Reilly, my editors at Crown, helped with the final stages of the project, offering a fresh outlook and perspective.

And finally, fond appreciation to Irene Prokop, editor and friend. Irene and her constantly costumed son, Kevin, were the inspiration for this book.

A NOTE TO PARENTS AND CAREGIVERS

Kids love costumes. Dressed up, their imaginations soar. They feel powerful, beautiful, enormous, tiny, hideous, cute, grown-up, ferocious, or cuddly. Whether it's Halloween, a school play, or a typical day at home, it's great fun to have an ample supply of costumes and props around the house.

Child's Play: Quick and Easy Costumes is a collection of costumes, props, and activities simple enough for everyday make-believe. Sewing and patterns have been avoided as much as possible, and the emphasis is on imaginative play, creativity, and a sense of humor.

These costumes should be fun to make as well as to wear. Seams and hems needn't be perfect. Fit needn't be exactly right. For outdoor use, make the costume roomy so your child can dress warmly underneath. The aim is for a safe and comfortable costume that sparks the imagination. Kids must be able to see, sit down, move around, and play.

Encourage your child to help create the costume idea and design by choosing paper or fabrics, coloring, painting, and making props and accessories. Often, kids can build an entire costume around one favorite prop. And don't forget to recycle costume pieces. Yesterday's supercape can become today's invisibility cloak!

SOME ITEMS YOU MAY WISH TO BUY

While most of the costumes in this book use supplies found around your home, a few props and accessories may be worth buying, to dress up or "finish" a homemade costume. Some items, certain hats or helmets for instance, are difficult to make. Purchased props often last for years and can be used in many costumes. Think about buying a limited supply of the following items:

- Shiny fabrics from your fabric store's remnant pile make wonderful and exotic capes.

- Garish yard sale jewelry adds sparkle to any fortune teller, gypsy, pirate, or royalty.

- A cowboy hat, plastic helmet (knight or motorcycle type), or similar piece of headwear will be used repeatedly over the years.

- An inexpensive, stiff paper eye mask held on the head with an elastic band will be used in dozens of costumes. Black is the most useful color, often seen on superheroes, Zorro, cats, ninja warriors, and burglars.

- Specific, one-of-a-kind props, such as vampire's fangs, add the perfect finishing touch.

Child's Play
Quick and Easy Costumes

NO-SEW COSTUMES

The costumes in this section use clothing and supplies that you've got around the house. They are great for a very young child, a last-minute costume, or an older child who wants to dress up with a minimum of fuss or effort.

The following suggestions will get you and your child started. Then find or make PROPS AND ACCESSORIES (page 121) to create the look you want.

You may want to stock up on the following frequently used supplies:

- Self-adhesive vinyl covering (sold in rolls or by the yard; available in hardware or department stores)

- *Water-soluble* white glue (the kind that says, "Washes out in soap and water" on the label)

- Washable markers

- Permanent markers

- Brightly colored plastic tape (comes in an assortment of colors; $\frac{1}{2}$-inch and 1-inch widths; available in hardware and variety stores)

THREE-HEADED MONSTER

You will need two pairs of old panty hose, two large, same-color balloons, safety pins, permanent markers, an oversize coat, and three hats to make this funny costume.

Inflate the balloons until each one is about the size of your child's head. Tie each balloon to seal it.

Place a balloon, knot down, in the top part of the panty hose, and close the top with a few safety pins. (1) Tie a knot in each leg of the panty hose, *as close to the balloon as possible.* (2) Repeat with second balloon and panty hose.

Use markers to draw faces and hair on each "head." Faces can be scary, silly, one happy/one sad, or plain. If balloon faces have special features, such as red cheeks or a mustache, add that makeup to child's face as well. Find three similar knit hats or baseball caps for the monster's three heads.

Attach the balloon heads to your child's shoulders by tying the panty hose legs around child's torso and under each arm. (3) Child wears oversize coat, zipped up to hold all three heads in place. Turning up the collar and adding a scarf makes the heads more stable.

★ *Note:* If Three-Headed Monster is planning to travel far from home, he/she might want to carry a spare balloon or two, in case of accidents!

Three pairs of sunglasses are a nice touch for daytime wear, but they will need to be taped to at least two of the heads.

An EXTRA ARM (page 146) is a particularly appropriate addition to this costume.

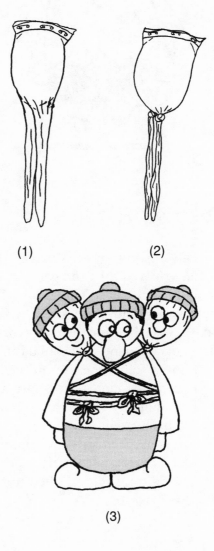

(1)   (2)

(3)

ONE-HEADED MONSTER

This simple and ugly costume uses your very shabbiest clothes. Child wears old, long-sleeved shirt and pants. Cut or tear the shirt-sleeves so that you have a ragged edge about 3 inches above the wrist. Cut or tear pants below the knee. If ragged clothes are unavailable, a dark, oversize shirt or coat worn with big winter gloves and heavy boots is a good start. Child can wear a down vest or a rolled-up bath towel under the shirt for wider shoulders.

Adding lots of hair gel or mousse to short hair helps create a spiky style. Long-haired monsters can tease their hair and use hair spray for a hideously bushy look.

The final touch is lots of green face makeup, with eyebrow pencil scars and stitches across forehead, neck, and cheeks. If desired, makeup and "stitches" can also be applied to exposed arms and legs. (See MAKEUP TIPS, page 164)

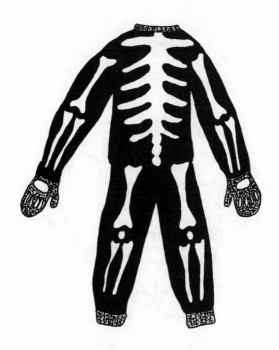

SKELETON

Using the illustration as a guide, cut bone shapes out of white felt.

Child wears black sweatsuit and black gloves or mittens. Glue "bones" to front of sweatsuit with *water-soluble* white glue (says "Washes out in soap and water" on label).

White face makeup with black circles around eyes or a purchased skeleton mask completes the costume.

★*Note:* When child is through with costume, peel bones off and launder sweatsuit as usual. Glue residue washes out.

Activity to try:

- If child shows an interest, find a picture of a real human skeleton. Talk about the functions and names of the bones. Use the picture as a guide for your costume.

MUMMY

Tear an old white sheet into strips about 2–4 inches wide. Child wears sweatsuit. Wrap arms, legs, and torso with sheet strips. Use safety pins (or a stitch or two) to fasten strip ends to sweatsuit. Leave some ends straggly. Wrap head with one or more long strips. White makeup with dark circles under or around eyes completes the look.

★ *Note:* For small children, you may want to use rolls of wide gauze bandage instead of sheet strips. Layered over a white or light gray sweatsuit, the look is very authentic. However, the bigger the child, the higher the cost.

GANGSTER/HENCHMAN

Gangsters wear mostly dark clothes, preferably black. For the "mean thug" look, child wears black or blue jeans, dark shirt or tank top, and a dark windbreaker or jean jacket, if available. Pad those powerful neck and arm muscles by rolling a bath towel lengthwise and placing it behind child's neck and along each arm. Use safety pins or masking tape to hold the towel in place on the child's shirt. Then cover the "muscles" with a jean jacket, zippered sweatshirt, or dark windbreaker.

Use mousse or gel to slick back or spike child's hair, and add dark sunglasses for a finishing touch. You may want to add an eyebrow pencil mustache or scar. A BURNT CORK BEARD (page 164) adds that "too nasty to shave" look. Your child may want to carry a purchased or homemade WEAPON (page 153). High-top sneakers or heavy boots complete the powerful thug costume.

SOPHISTICATED MOBSTER

For the more sophisticated mobster, try to find black pants and a black, button-up shirt. Cut a simple thin, white necktie out of fabric or heavy paper. Tie or safety-pin necktie to shirt. An old, dark suit jacket is a nice touch.

Accessories include a man's hat worn low over one eye and a thin eyebrow pencil mustache. Mobsters usually carry large amounts of pretend cash to bribe people, and they often conceal WEAPONS (page 153) under their clothes.

★ *Note:* The Sophisticated Mobster and the Gangster/Henchman make a very intimidating duo when traveling together.

NINJA WARRIOR

The ninja warrior is covered completely in black. A black sweatsuit is fine, with a black sash belt tied around the waist. Child can wear a black ski mask that covers forehead, nose, and mouth; a black HOOD (page 128); or a black headband with BURNT CORK MAKEUP (page 164) covering his or her entire face.

Ninjas tuck their pant legs into soft black boots. If available, tuck child's pants into heavy, black socks.

Ninjas also carry a good supply of NINJA WEAPONS (page 161).

MARTIAL ARTIST

Child wears white pants and white, long-sleeved shirt or robe with a black fabric belt around the waist. For extra color, tie bright red scarves (made from scrap fabric) just above knees and elbows. Tie a bright red scarf around child's head, leaving the ends long.

For indoor play, child should be barefoot.

PIRATE

This costume is a great way to use up torn clothes—the shabbier the better. Child wears a plain or striped shirt and old pants. Sweatpants or jeans are fine, cut raggedly just below the knee, to make knickers. Tie a bright sash around waist for belt, or use a plain belt with a big buckle. A dark-colored QUICKIE VEST (page 106) is optional.

Make an EYE PATCH by stitching a circle of black felt to a length of thin, black elastic.

Child wears a PIRATE'S EARRING (page 134) and TRIANGLE KERCHIEF (page 131).

Tuck a SWORD or DAGGER (page 156) into belt.

A BURNT CORK BEARD (page 164), eyebrow pencil scar on cheek, and nasty sneer complete the look.

Activities to try:

- Pirates often have a pirate accent and say things like "Aye, matey, it's time to walk the plank!" or "Shiver me timbers! It's land ho!"

- Children might like to draw their own map of a desert island, complete with trails, mountains, dark caves, dangerous traps, and buried treasure.

- Hide a small snack or other treat, and supply clues for pirates to follow.

MOTORCYCLE RIDER

This tough-looking costume calls for black or blue jeans, black T-shirt, and a black or blue QUICKIE VEST (page 106) or jean jacket. Make a motorcycle emblem from felt, and attach to back of vest or jacket with *water-soluble* white glue (says "Washes out in soap and water" on label).

Decorate child's arms with washable marker tattoos. A BURNT CORK BEARD (page 164), kerchief headband, and sunglasses complete this dangerous look.

SIMPLE SUPERHERO

For a simple and instant costume, child wears a solid-color shirt and a NO-SEW CAPE (page 111) or bath towel cape. Draw the appropriate superhero emblem on a white paper plate or piece of stiff paper (see EMBLEM TEMPLATES, page 135). Color the emblem with markers, cut it out, and tape it to the front of the shirt with loops of masking tape.

Child wears colored tights with contrasting color kneesocks over them.

Make a belt and wristbands out of lengths of aluminum foil, folded a few times for thickness and strength, and taped closed. Other accessories might include an aluminum foil or paper headband, GLOVES (page 145), or a MASK (page 122).

Use colored plastic tape on child's shirt for added details such as stripes, bands, and other uniform designs.

✱ *Note:* For more elaborate SUPERHERO costumes, and for ACTIVITIES TO TRY, see pages 118–19 in the FABRIC section.

ROCK STAR

Rock stars have many styles, from outrageous to ordinary. Child can choose a flashy, shiny look with a leotard top, Lycra tights or shorts, homemade jewelry, and lots of makeup. Or go for the grungy look with ripped jeans, ripped T-shirt, old flannel shirt, and bandana headband.

Use mousse or gel to create spiky hairstyles, if desired.

Make a life-size cutout of a guitar from heavy cardboard, and decorate with paints or markers. Hang around neck with ribbon or old necktie.

HIPPIE/FLOWER CHILD

Return to the '60s with a costume of faded or ripped jeans covered with bright fabric patches. An India-print shirt, plain shirt, or T-shirt picturing a favorite rock band is great. Girls can wear India-print skirts and blouses. A QUICKIE VEST with long fringe is a nice touch (page 106). Child wears sandals, beach thongs, sneakers, or work boots.

Simple bead necklaces are fun to make and are the perfect hippie jewelry. Child can also make paper peace sign buttons (see illustration). Attach to shirt or vest with a loop of tape.

Part child's hair down the middle, and tie a headband or bandana around head. Girls can wear long, dangly earrings.

FORTUNE TELLER

Girls wear brightly colored blouses and long, flowing skirts. Tie a colorful scarf around child's waist for a belt, and add another scarf on head (see TRIANGLE KERCHIEF, page 131). A long shawl, loads of jewelry (see FOIL BEAD NECKLACE, page 132), and heavy makeup complete the look.

Boys wear bright shirts and dark pants. Add a QUICKIE VEST (page 106), a bright scarf belt, and a TRIANGLE KERCHIEF (page 131) or towel turban. A BURNT CORK BEARD (page 164) is a nice touch.

"Crystal ball" can be a play ball wrapped in aluminum foil, covered with plastic wrap, and secured with clear tape.

Activities to try:

- Children can gaze into the future and come up with amazing predictions:

  "You will get wet sometime in the next two days."
  "I see chocolate chip cookies in the very near future."
  "You will sneeze at least three times this week."
  "Our family will go on a short trip very soon and eat something sweet."

- Fortune tellers might like to bake muffins with a written fortune folded in foil and hidden inside each muffin!

WIRE-WING BUTTERFLY

Child wears black clothing (leotard and tights; sweatsuit; T-shirt and shorts), WIRE WINGS (page 148–50), and ANTENNAE (page 144). Use white or colored panty hose or tights to make the wings, decorating them with bright fabric designs. Stitch fabric pieces in place, or attach with a hot glue gun.

★ *Note:* See also CIRCLE BUTTERFLY, page 101.

ALADDIN

Make a short QUICKIE VEST (page 106) with rounded edges, as shown. Child wears vest over tank top, T-shirt, or bare chest. Baggy sweatpants are perfect, with a wide sash belt. Complete the look with a bath towel turban (held in place with a safety pin and decorated with a paper "jewel") and aluminum foil armbands around upper arms.

Activities to try:

• Every home has a flying carpet hidden away somewhere. Try a bath mat or towel, tied at the corners with yarn.

• A plastic dish detergent bottle can be transformed into a magic lamp with some gold spray paint and colorful paper jewels.

LUMBERJACK

Lumberjacks wear flannel or woolen shirts and jeans tucked into heavy boots. Hiking boots, rain boots, or snow boots are fine. These are very muscular people, so a sweatshirt or two, worn *under* the shirt for warmth, makes for a more authentic look. Suspenders, a down vest, a knit hat, and a BURNT CORK BEARD (page 164) complete the costume.

Activity to try:

- Make an authentic lumberjack's AXE (see page 158 in PROPS section).

POLICE OFFICER

Props and accessories are the most important part of this costume. Child wears dark shirt and pants (navy blue shirt and blue jeans are good). Make a cardboard badge, cover it with aluminum foil, and decorate it with permanent marker. Tape the badge to child's shirt with a loop of masking tape.

Child can wear a baseball cap with an aluminum foil emblem or badge taped over cap emblem. A purchased or homemade RAY GUN (page 163) and WALKIE-TALKIE (see below) complete the effect.

Activities to try:

- Use empty bank check boxes ($3\frac{1}{2} \times 7$ inches) to make authentic-looking BOX WALKIE-TALKIES. Cover each box with black cloth tape or paper, and add paper or foil buttons, speakers, and dials. Attach a pipe cleaner as an antenna.

- Young children might like to make PAPER CUP WALKIE-TALKIES. Use a pencil point to punch a small hole in the bottom of two paper cups. Thread a long string through the cups, as shown, and knot each end so the string won't pull out. Children hold cups and walk apart until string is taut but not touching any corners or furniture.

Send and receive messages by alternately speaking into and listening in cup.

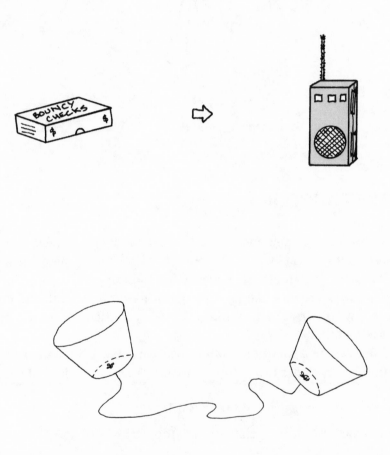

FIRE FIGHTER

Child wears raincoat and boots. Fire hat can be purchased, or wear a baseball cap backwards, decorated with a foil emblem in front. Some fire departments give plastic fire hats away.

   Make a cardboard badge, cover it with aluminum foil, and decorate it with permanent marker. Tape it to raincoat with a loop of masking tape.

   Hose can be a vacuum cleaner hose, cardboard gift-wrap tube, or a number of paper towel tubes threaded on a long piece of string.

Activities to try:

- Practice fire safety behavior of "Stop, Drop, and Roll."

- Child or adult can organize a family fire drill. Evacuate the house in record time, and gather at a predetermined "safe spot."

COWBOY/COWGIRL

Child wears jeans, flannel shirt, QUICKIE VEST with fringe (page 106), and purchased cowboy hat (or old hat with yarn around crown and under chin). Girls may choose to wear skirts with FRINGE (see NATIVE AMERICAN, page 22) attached to bottom hem.

A sheriff's badge can be cut from thin cardboard, covered with aluminum foil, and decorated with permanent marker. Attach it to vest with a loop of masking tape. Tie a bandana loosely around child's neck. A small coil of rope hanging from child's belt might come in handy for chasing down stray cows.

If desired, a purchased or homemade RAY GUN (page 163) completes the look.

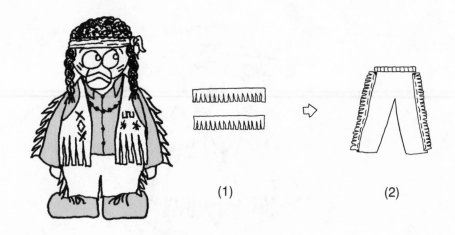

(1)   (2)

NATIVE AMERICAN

Child wears brown pants (or jeans), shirt (if weather is cool), and a tan or brown fringed QUICKIE VEST (page 106). Tie a kerchief around head for headband, or make a PAPER HEADBAND as shown in PAPER BAG NATIVE AMERICAN (page 38). Decorate the vest with NATIVE AMERICAN SYMBOLS AND DESIGNS (page 39). Either draw designs with marker or cut them out of felt and glue them to the vest with white or fabric glue.

For an authentic look, add FRINGE to child's clothing. Cut long strips of brown fabric, 2–3 inches wide, and cut fringe as shown. (1) Baste or safety pin fringe to outside of pants (2) and shirtsleeves, and across upper back of vest.

Girls may want to wear long, fringed NO-SEW TUNICS (page 103), made out of tan material and decorated with NATIVE AMERICAN SYMBOLS AND DESIGNS (page 39).

Use lipstick or eyebrow pencil to decorate child's face. If desired, child can carry BOW AND ARROWS (page 155) and QUIVER (page 155).

Activity to try:

• Make Native American jewelry by stringing beads or making a FOIL BEAD NECKLACE (page 132).

MOUNTAIN CLIMBER

This costume is especially good for cold weather outdoor play. Child wears a turtleneck, heavy sweater or sweatshirt, long pants or knickers (cut from old sweatpants), and kneesocks. If it's cold, a down vest looks good. Hiking boots are ideal, although sneakers or boots of any kind are fine.

Other accessories include a knit hat, gloves, and sunglasses for high-altitude snowfields. Child wears a backpack and carries a coil of rope and a homemade Ice Axe (see below).

Activity to try:

- Make an Ice Axe. Make the ice axe blade by squashing the ends of a paper towel tube, so that one end is flat and horizontal, and the other end is flat and vertical, as shown on page 24. (1) If a hot glue gun is available, squirt some glue inside the tube ends to stabilize the shape and flatten the blades.

  Cover both blade ends with silver duct tape. Cut jagged "teeth" in the vertical end, as shown. (2) Use scissors to trim top edge of toothed end to be a bit rounded. (2) If necessary, close any opened edges with more hot glue or duct tape. Cut a

1½-inch slit in the bottom of the blade, as shown in Figure 2.

To make the ice axe handle, roll at least ten pages of newspaper together into a tight roll about 1¼ inches in diameter. Wrap this roll with black cloth tape (available in hardware stores) or two to three layers of masking tape. The handle should be at least 16 inches long and sturdy. (3)

Push one end of the handle into the slit in the bottom of the blade. Use either black or silver tape to attach the handle to the blade, as shown. (4) Cover the rest of the blade with silver duct tape.

Insert a pointed piece of cardboard into the bottom of the handle. Attach it to the handle, and cover it with silver duct tape. (4)

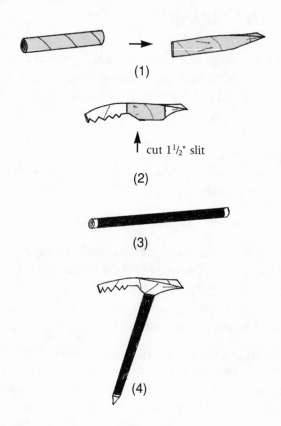

(1)

cut 1½" slit

(2)

(3)

(4)

POLITICIAN

Child wears conservative dress clothes, or can decide to have a trademark outfit (jogging clothes, overalls, etc.).

Props and demeanor are most important parts of this costume. Child wears an oversize "Vote for <u>Child's Name</u>" button and hands out fliers listing election promises (see below for suggestions). If a copy machine is available, fliers can even feature child's picture.

This costume comes in handy during school elections or during election years.

Activity to try:

- Child can make up slogans, design buttons, and write pamphlets listing his or her platform. It's fun to hire a "campaign manager" to help with the creation and distribution of election materials.

Some popular election promises:

Later bedtimes
Bigger desserts
Longer weekends
Birthdays twice a year

ATHLETE

(This is an instant costume for last-minute emergencies.)

Child wears sports uniform from a sport that he, she, or an older sibling plays. Or cut a large number out of felt, and glue it on child's shirt or sweatshirt with *water-soluble* white glue (says "Washes out in soap and water" on label). Child can carry equipment or ball appropriate to the sport (e.g., football, soccer ball, tennis racquet).

When costume is no longer needed, peel felt number off, and launder shirt as usual. Glue residue will wash out.

Make a gold MEDALLION (page 134) if ATHLETE has just returned from the Olympics.

CHEERLEADER

Child wears a dark skirt or pants with a white or light-colored sweater or sweatshirt. Cut out a large team letter or emblem from brightly colored felt and glue it to the sweatshirt front with water-soluble white glue (says "Washes out in soap and water" on label). Child wears white socks and sneakers and carries a poster board MEGAPHONE (see below) or purchased pom-poms.

When costume is no longer needed, peel letter off sweater and launder as usual. Glue residue will wash out.

Activities to try:

- To make a MEGAPHONE, use white or colored poster board. (A color to match the felt team letter is a nice touch.) From a 9 × 9–inch square, cut out the shape shown in Figure 1. Run poster board shape along a table edge to curve it gently. Form it into a cone shape, with a 1½-inch opening at the small end, and secure seams with masking tape, inside and out. (2)

Cut a second piece of poster board, 1 × 6 inches, for handle. Fold the piece lengthwise, and wrap it with masking tape. (3)

Attach handle, running masking tape completely around megaphone. (4)

- This is a good time to practice cartwheels, jumping jacks, and general aerobic dancing.

- Your cheerleader can make up some original cheers to show enthusiasm for family members, friends, favorite TV characters, or even a favorite food:

  "Gimme a T! Gimme an O! Gimme an F!
  Gimme a U! What does it spell? . . ."

MEGAPHONE INSTRUCTIONS

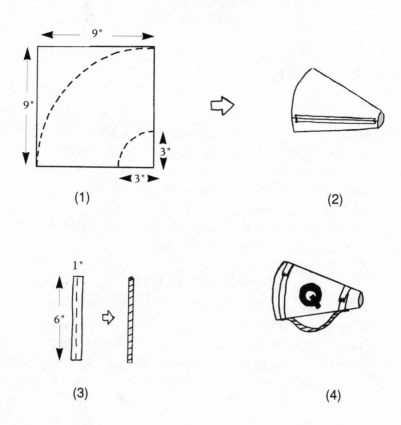

TWINS

This is a fun and easy costume for two friends or siblings to do together. Children decide on a simple outfit that they both own. Try blue jeans, white T-shirt, gray sweatshirt, and a baseball cap. Each child can carry a matching prop (identical footballs, identical dolls or stuffed animals).

Activities to try:

- When trick-or-treating, TWINS approach door together and yell "Trick or treat!" and "Thank you!" in unison.

- Older children might want to try mirror acting. TWINS face each other, or stand side by side, and make slow, identical movements. This is especially fun to do at mealtime.

BACKWARDS BOY/BACKWARDS GIRL

Child wears clothing backwards. Help your child to button shirts up the back and put pants on backwards. A baseball cap on backwards is great.

For a backwards man, a necktie or bow tie worn backwards is a nice effect. A backwards woman can wear a long bead necklace down her back, and maybe a backwards belt with a flashy buckle.

If desired, a homemade or purchased full-face mask can be worn on the *back* of child's head. Hide the top of the mask with a hat.

Activities to try:

- For trick-or-treating, child walks backwards, guided by an adult or older child, extending trick-or-treat bag behind him or her.

- At home, backwards children do many things backwards: read a short book from end to beginning; have a (small) dessert before the rest of the meal; say "Excuse me!" and then burp!

BABY

(This costume is funniest on older children.)

Child wears borrowed baby bonnet or floppy hat, T-shirt or sweatshirt, bib (borrowed or homemade), and diaper worn *over* tights or pants. Use a real, large-size diaper or a hand towel, pinned at the sides with large safety pins. Buy a pacifier, and hang it around child's neck with a ribbon. Child can carry a rattle, plastic bottle, doll, or stuffed animal.

DALMATIAN

Child wears white sweatsuit, white shirt and pants, white leotard and tights, or some combination of these. Cut circles out of black felt. Circles can be 1–2 inches across. Use *water-soluble* white glue (says "Washes out in soap and water" on label) to attach dots to outfit. Apply white and black makeup to add spots, whiskers, and a black nose to child's face.

If desired, make white fabric HOOD (page 128), FLOPPY EARS (page 142), and FABRIC TAIL (page 153), and glue black spots to these also. Attach tail with safety pin or a few stitches.

Child can make a "dog tag" out of stiff paper or cardboard to wear around neck on a loose ribbon.

When costume is no longer needed, peel black dots off clothes and launder as usual. Glue residue washes out.

Activity to try:

- Your new pet may enjoy learning some doggy tricks. Teach your Dalmatian to sit, stay, come, beg, shake hands, roll over, play dead, and speak. Advanced tricks might be "Fetch the ball!" (without using hands), or "Go get Daddy!" (without speaking).

JACK AND THE BEANSTALK

Child wears an oversize, solid-color T-shirt (or a NO-SEW TUNIC, page 103) over a turtleneck, with a belt or sash around waist. Put a few dried beans in pants pocket. Use safety pins to attach a length of plastic or silk ivy from left shoulder to right hip.

Activity to try:

- Dried beans sprout and grow very quickly. Your child may want to plant a few in paper cups to grow a beanstalk at home.

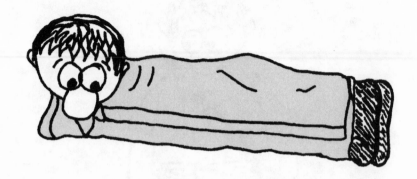

GIANT WORM OR SNAKE

This is an easy and instant costume for adult-supervised indoor play. Child rolls up in a sheet or blanket and slithers along the floor.

PAPER BAG COSTUMES

Paper bag costumes are quick and easy for very young children, ages two to four. Disposable and temporary, they lend themselves to lots of creative and imaginative play. If you like, reinforce armholes and neck edges with nylon strapping tape or duct tape, and these costumes will last for weeks.

The supplies needed for the following costumes include:

- Brown paper grocery bags
- Scissors
- Masking tape
- Markers or crayons
- Aluminum foil
- Lots of imagination.

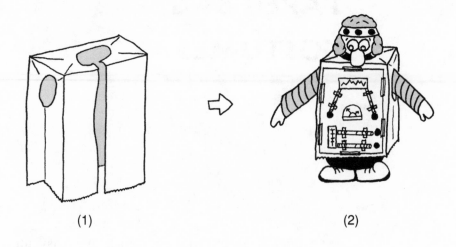

(1)   (2)

PAPER BAG ROBOT

Slit grocery bag up the middle of the large blank side. Cut a neck hole in the bottom of bag, and armholes in the sides. (1)

Cover front of bag with aluminum foil, and secure with masking tape. Then you and your child can decorate bag with robot buttons, switches, and dials. Use milk bottle caps attached with loops of tape for buttons; drinking straws make great tubing; draw and color paper dials and switches. (2)

Make an aluminum foil headband, decorated with paper dials or milk bottle caps. For stiff robot arms, slit two paper towel tubes lengthwise. Decorate with crayon or marker and put over child's arms. (2)

Activities to try:

- Young robots speak in a simple, flat "robot voice."

- Give your robot some kitchen tongs to pick up, carry, and drop objects. Then ask your robot to carry out simple tasks such as:

    "Pick up that red sock and put it on the bed."
    "Pick up all the little blocks and put them in this box."
    "Go tell everyone that it is snack time."

ASTRONAUT

Follow the directions for ROBOT, but decorate with more dials and fewer buttons. Add some paper NASA emblems. Omit stiff robot arms, but child might want to wear a sweatsuit under costume because it's very cold in space. Astronauts also wear oversize gloves.

From a smaller paper bag, make a simple ASTRONAUT HELMET, as shown (see page 44). Cover it with aluminum foil, securing with masking tape. Decorate helmet with NASA insignia on sides and child's name on front.

Activities to try:

- Look at books about space, rockets, planets, and stars. Talk about which planets might be fun to visit, and what supplies would be good to take along.

- Draw pictures of planets, rockets, astronauts, and aliens.

- Make a spaceship out of a large cardboard box or a blanket tent.

- Fill a backpack with supplies for an adventure in space: stuffed animal, favorite book, flashlight, and a snack.

PAPER BAG NATIVE AMERICAN

Cut a 2-inch strip from the top of a grocery bag to make a HEAD-BAND. (1) Measure and cut it to fit your child's head. Decorate the headband with NATIVE AMERICAN SYMBOLS AND DESIGNS (opposite) and feathers cut from construction paper. Then tape securely to fit child's head.

To make a vest, slit the bag up the middle of the printed side. Cut off the bottom of the bag so you have a long rectangle. (2)

Trim the rectangle to about 34 × 15 inches. With printing on the bag facing up, fold the ends in to meet in the middle.

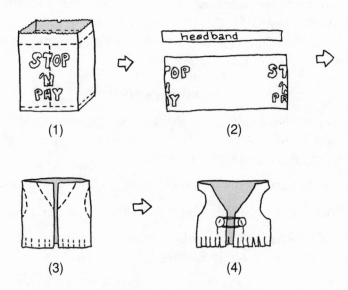

(1)   (2)

(3)   (4)

Cut armholes along each fold, about 2 inches from the top of the bag. Cut a V-shape in the front of the vest. Cut fringe along the bottom edge. (3)

To make simple buttons, cut two paper circles, about 1½ inches in diameter, from bag scraps. Staple the buttons to the front of the vest, as shown in Figure 4. Loosely wind a bit of yarn or string around the buttons to hold the vest closed.

Use markers or crayons to decorate the vest with NATIVE AMERICAN SYMBOLS AND DESIGNS (below). Eyebrow pencil or lipstick "face paint" completes the look.

Activity to try:

• Use an old blanket or sheet to erect an indoor tent. A blanket or sleeping bag on the floor makes this a cozy place for a snack, a good book, or a nap.

NATIVE AMERICAN SYMBOLS AND DESIGNS

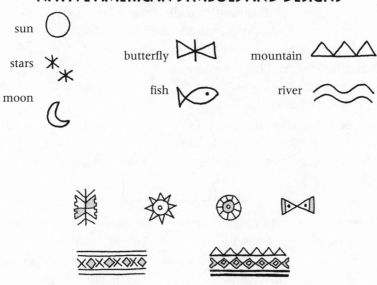

sun

stars

moon

butterfly

fish

mountain

river

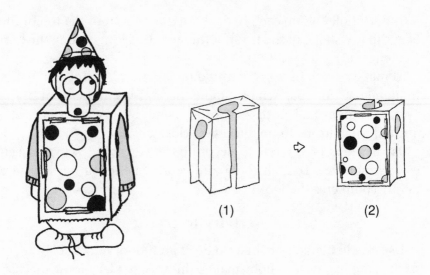

(1)   (2)

CLOWN

Slit grocery bag up the middle of the large blank side. Cut a neck hole in the bottom of the bag, and armholes in the sides. (1)

Cover the printed front of bag with white paper, taping all edges with masking tape. Then cover white paper with large polka dots (2–3 inches in diameter). Dots can be made with colorful paper cutouts, markers, or crayons. (2)

Complete the costume with a Cone Hat (page 125) or a wacky-looking Paper Plate Hat (page 124).

If desired, use lipstick to color child's nose and cheeks.

Activity to try:

• Clowns and young children have a lot in common. When they try to juggle, the balls fly all over. When they make a tower of blocks, they accidentally knock it down. They read books upside down and say silly things. But when your child is dressed as a clown, these things are *extra* funny.

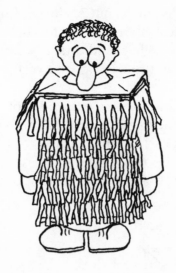

SHAGGY MONSTER

You will need two paper grocery bags for this costume. Slit one bag up the middle of the large blank side. Cut a neck hole in the bottom of the bag and armholes in the sides. (1) Reinforce neck and armholes with nylon strapping tape or duct tape.

From the second paper bag, cut five rectangles measuring 6 × 12 inches. Stack them together, and crumple them up into a ball. When the paper is completely crumpled, spread the sheets out again, in a crumpled stack. Cut through all five sheets, every ½ inch or so, as shown in Figure 2, to make long, shaggy fringe.

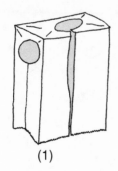

(1)

(2)

Separate sheets. Measure about 3½ inches from the bottom front of the first bag. Use clear tape to attach a row of fringe at this point. (3) Measure 3½ inches higher, and attach a second row of fringe. Continue until the entire front of the costume is covered with fringe. (4)

If desired, repeat this process with sides of bag. You will need three rows of fringe below each armhole, and one row of fringe at the top, overlapping each armhole. (5)

This is a very shaggy, rustly-sounding costume for young monsters. A messy hairstyle and a fierce expression complete the look.

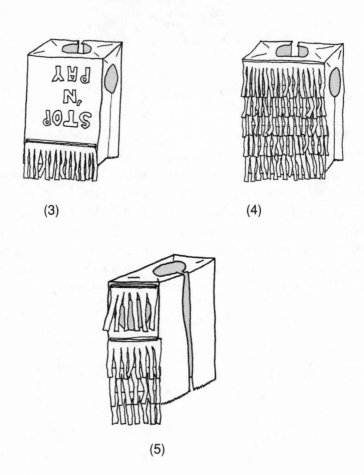

(3)   (4)

(5)

PAPER BAG KNIGHT

Slit grocery bag up the middle of the large blank side. Cut a neck hole in the bottom of the bag, and armholes in the sides. (1)

For that "knight in shining armor" look, cover front and sides of bag with aluminum foil, taping all edges with masking tape. Use permanent marker to draw a simple COAT OF ARMS design on the front of the foil (see examples, Figure 2). Or, for a more elaborate costume, draw a colorful coat of arms on white paper, cut it out, and tape it to the front of the costume.

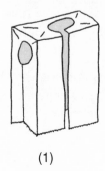

(1)

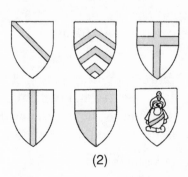

(2)

Child can wear a purchased helmet, or you can make a PAPER BAG KNIGHT'S HELMET. Use a bag that fits closely over child's head. Trim bottom of bag so that when child wears helmet, bag edges come to shoulders. Put bag on child's head, and lightly mark where to trim front of helmet, as shown in Figure 3. Cover helmet with aluminum foil, taping all edges. If desired, decorate front of helmet with a colorful paper plume.

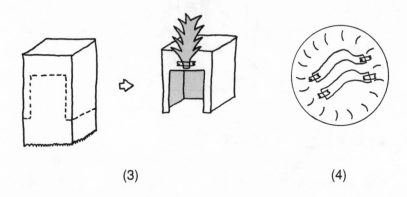

(3)   (4)

Activities to try:

- A quick sword can be made from a flattened paper towel tube covered in aluminum foil. Wrap one end with masking tape to form a handle. See also DAGGERS AND SWORDS, page 156.

- To make a PAPER PLATE SHIELD, ask your child to decorate the *bottom* of a paper plate with a colorful design. Cut two strips from a second plate, about $1\frac{1}{2} \times 8$ inches. Use masking tape to secure the strip ends to the inside of the plate, as shown in Figure 4, to serve as the shield's handle.

  A more authentic looking shield can be made using the above technique with a lightweight aluminum pie tin. Tape a COAT OF ARMS design to the bottom of the tin, and make a handle using masking tape and paper plate strips.

  See also SHIELDS, page 159.

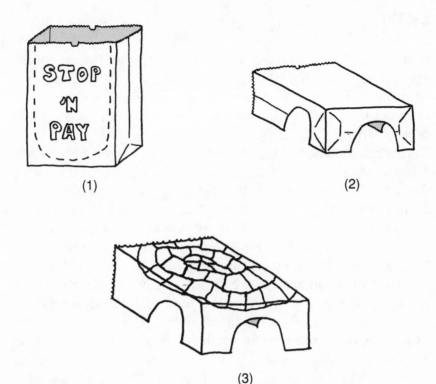

(1)

(2)

(3)

PAPER BAG TURTLE

Use a bag with printing on only one side. Cut off the side of the bag with printing on it. (1)

Cut a U-shaped hole in the bottom of the bag for the child's neck. Then cut U-shaped holes in the sides of the bag for child's shoulders, as shown. (2)

Use marker or crayon to draw a turtle-shell pattern on the blank side of the bag. (3)

Child wears costume while on hands and knees, crawling slowly! Tape sides of bag to child's shirt to secure, if necessary.

Activities to try:

- Read a book about turtles, and act out part of the story.

- A pair of turtles can have a race to see who is slower.

LION

Find a bag with printing on only one side. Cut off the side of the bag with printing on it. (1)

Cut a U-shaped hole in the bottom of the bag for the child's neck. Then cut U-shaped holes in the sides of the bag for child's shoulders, as shown. (2)

From a second paper bag, cut out two circles about 12 inches in diameter. Stack circles with printed sides together, and crumple into a ball. Then flatten out and cut fringe around outer edge to make lion's mane. (3) Use loops of masking tape to tape circles together in center. Use more loops of tape to attach mane to neck area, allowing about 6 inches of mane to extend above bag. Cut U-shaped neck hole in mane, to match neck hole in bag. (4)

Cut a strip of paper, $1\frac{1}{2} \times 12$ inches long, widening at one end, as shown in Figure 4. Crumple the wide end, flatten it, and cut fringe to make a tail. Tape tail to end of bag.

Child wears costume while on hands and knees. Tape sides of bag to child's shirt to secure, if necessary. Child can wear tan or brown socks on hands for paws. If desired, use paper scraps to make PERKY EARS (page 142), and add eyebrow pencil whiskers and nose for a finishing touch.

Activities to try:

- This lion is very fierce and growls a great deal, but can probably be trained to crawl through a hoop or roll a ball.

- Lions often like to make their dens under tables.

- Some lions like cages made from large cardboard boxes. Use sharp scissors or a heavy knife to cut bars on two sides of the box.

(1)

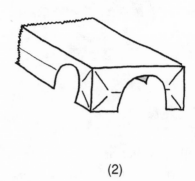

(2)

(3)

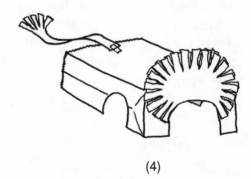

(4)

TIGER

Follow directions for Lion, but omit mane and round end of tail, as shown. Use markers, crayons, or poster paint to draw orange and black stripes on Tiger's back, sides, and tail.

ZEBRA

Follow directions for Lion, but make Zebra mane. From a paper bag scrap, cut a rectangle 5 × 7 inches. (1) Fold in half the long way, and cut fringe. (2) Tape both sides of the folded edge to the costume, using masking tape. (3)

Use markers, crayons, or poster paint to draw white and black stripes on Zebra's body. Paint or color the mane solid black.

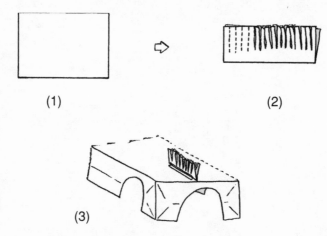

(1)　　　　　　　　　　　(2)

(3)

SANDWICH BOARD COSTUMES

to make these simple costumes you will need one or two large pieces of cardboard or poster board, markers or poster paints, and ribbon. Poster board is available at supermarkets, drugstores, or stationery stores, and comes in a variety of colors. Other supplies might include spray paint, colored plastic tape (available at hardware stores), duct tape, aluminum foil, and various props.

Adjust the size of the costume to fit your child. It should be short enough for walking to be easy.

A nice feature of sandwich board costumes is that they are easily removed to play games or eat refreshments. When your child is through with the costume, think about mounting it on a bedroom or playroom wall.

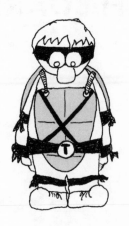
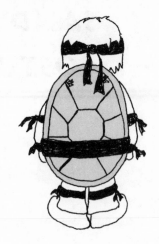

WARRIOR TURTLE

To make the back shell, measure from the base of your child's neck to just below his or her bottom, and add an inch. Find a piece of corrugated cardboard that is roughly this long and wide enough to make a shell-shaped oval. Copy the pattern shown in Figure 1 onto the cardboard, and cut it out.

Use a razor knife to lightly score the inside octagon shape. (*Scoring* means cutting through just the top layer of cardboard. Do *not* cut all the way through!) (2)

Use heavy scissors to cut along the remaining lines. (2)

Cut *slivers*, as shown in Figure 3, out of each section along the cut

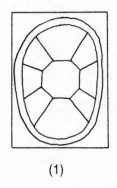

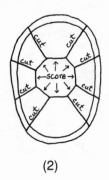

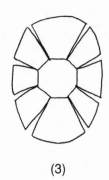

(1)   (2)   (3)

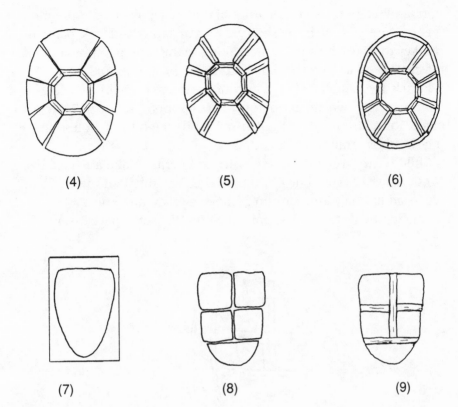

(4)   (5)   (6)

(7)   (8)   (9)

lines. The bigger the slivers, the more of a curved shape the shell will have.

Bend each section of cardboard down at the scored line, and cover the bent seam with duct tape. (4)

Use duct tape to join the cut sections tightly. As you tape, the convex shell shape will form. (5)

Hold shell up to child's back. If shell is too large, trim outer edge. Run duct tape along the outer edge, folding tape over as you go. (6)

Paint or spray-paint both sides of shell either brown or dark green, and allow to dry. Use black paint or permanent marker to draw the shell design along seams.

Front turtle shell is smaller. Cut the shape in Figure 7 out of a second piece of cardboard.

Cut into slightly rounded sections, as shown. (8) Tape the sections together on both sides with duct tape. (9) (Cutting into sections and retaping makes the front of the shell look more authentic!)

Paint one side of front shell yellow or tan. Use black paint or marker to draw the shell design along seams. Use paint or colored plastic tape to add crossed straps to chest area, if desired.

Punch two small holes in top of back shell, about 7–8 inches apart. Punch two holes in top of front shell, about 6–7 inches apart. Run dark brown or green ribbon through these holes, making shoulder straps. (10)

Child wears green or brown shirt and tights. Make a FABRIC EYE MASK (page 123), and tie a wide sash belt around both shells. Child wears additional sashes around elbows, wrists, and knees.

Warrior Turtles carry a supply of NINJA WEAPONS (page 161).

(10)

Activity to try:

• Make a miniature version of this costume for a favorite stuffed animal. Using either cardboard or poster board, follow the directions above to create a "Ninja Bear" or "Warrior Teddy."

ROAD SIGN

Your child can choose the road sign he or she wants to be (see below). Use one piece of colored poster board, or spray-paint a large piece of cardboard the color you want. Cut out the desired shape, and use poster paint, markers, or colored plastic tape to add the lettering and border.

Punch two holes in top of sign, centered and about 8–10 inches apart. Attach about 20 inches of ribbon, and hang around child's neck.

 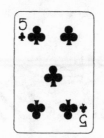 

PLAYING CARD

Use two pieces of poster board for this costume, one white and one colored. Slightly round all corners to resemble a playing card shape. Decorate the colored poster board as the back of the playing card, drawing a simple pattern, as shown, or copying the back of a real card.

Using a playing card as your guide, draw the card design on the white piece of poster board. An ace or low number is easiest to copy. You might suggest your child's age as the number of the card, and your child can pick the suit. For example, a six-year-old could be the six of diamonds. A diamond, heart, club, or spade template, made from stiff paper, will make your design look more consistent.

Punch holes in the top of poster board pieces, centered and about 7–9 inches apart. Then attach lengths of ribbon and hang over child's shoulders.

Activities to try:

- While you've got the cards out, try some games of Go Fish, Old Maid, or Rummy.

- When you're tired of card games, don't forget to build a few card towers and castles. A carpet or tablecloth makes a good rough surface to work on.

ROCKET SHIP

Use two pieces of white poster board, or use cardboard, painted white or silver. The following instructions are for poster board, 22 × 28 inches.

Cut out rocket shapes, as shown. (1) Save the scraps to use later. Cut a 10-inch slit in the center bottom of each rocket. (1)

From scraps of poster board, cut two "fins," as shown in Figure 2. Fold over ½ inch on the long side of each fin, as shown on page 56. (3)

Insert fold inside slit, and tape securely on each side of fin and on inside of rocket. (4)

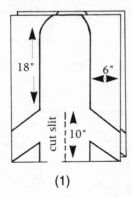

(1)

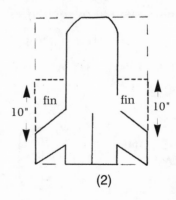

(2)

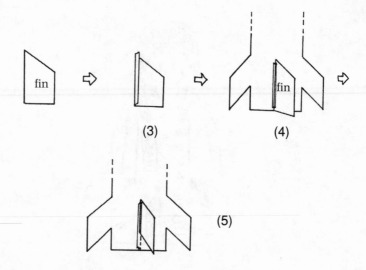

(3)   (4)

(5)

Trim three-dimensional fin to match the shape of the side fins. (5)
Decorate rocket with USA and NASA emblems. Punch holes in
top of rocket, about 6 inches apart, and attach ribbon to hang over
child's shoulders.

Activities to try:

- Make a NOSE CONE HELMET to complete the outer space look. Cut
  a helmet shape out of a clean plastic, 1-gallon milk or water jug
  (see below). Be careful to round all edges and check for rough
  spots. Leave helmet plain, or give it more of a nose cone look
  with silver or gray spray paint, or silver duct tape. Decorate with
  USA or NASA emblems. Depending on the size of your child,
  helmet will fit over child's head or sit above ears.

- Make a CONE HAT (page 125) out of silver or gray paper.

- Make a PAPER BAG ASTRONAUT HELMET (page 37).

**NOSE CONE
HELMET**

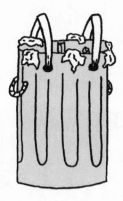

GARBAGE CAN

Securely tape two pieces of green or gray poster board together to form a cylinder, as shown below. Adjust size of cylinder to fit your child, trimming off extra poster board.

Decorate outside of "can" with lines, pipe cleaner handles, and bits of paper "garbage" glued or taped to the top edge.

Or create a recycling can by writing a slogan on the outside, such as "Recycle Today! Cans and Bottles Only!" or "Recycle Today! Candy Only!"

Punch holes, front and back, about 7–9 inches apart, and attach ribbon for shoulder straps.

Activity to try:

- A GARBAGE CAN costume can be the centerpiece for a game of Garbage Toss. Take off the costume, and set it on the floor. Children stand at a distance and take turns tossing crumpled balls of newspaper or other paper trash into the can.

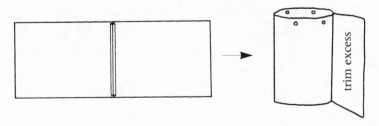

trim excess

SODA CAN

Follow instructions for GARBAGE CAN, (page 57) but use white poster board. Use paint and markers to draw design and logo of child's favorite soda, canned drink, or canned food. (It is easiest to sketch the design in pencil, lay the poster board flat again, and paint or draw your design on a flat surface.)

Cover a paper towel or gift-wrap tube with white paint or paper. Wind a strip of red plastic tape around the tube, or draw a red stripe with markers or paint. Tape this "straw" to inside of can.

CRAYON

Follow instructions for GARBAGE CAN but use poster board in child's favorite color. Use paint or markers to draw the design and logo of a crayon. Make a CONE HAT (page 125) for the crayon point out of leftover poster board pieces.

Child can wear clothing and face makeup to match the crayon color.

TUBE OF TOOTHPASTE

Cut two pieces of white poster board into long rectangles, about 15 × 28 inches. Use markers and poster paint to draw a facsimile of a toothpaste tube, front and back. Punch holes in the top of poster board pieces, and attach ribbon to hang over child's shoulders.

Use the leftover poster board pieces to make a cap for your toothpaste tube. Cut a rectangle about 7 × 22 inches. Bring the ends together, and tape so cap fits child's head and is slightly cone shaped. Trim any uneven edges. Draw vertical lines on cap with black marker. Punch two holes in bottom sides of cap, and attach ribbon to tie under child's chin.

Child can carry a toothbrush as a prop, or you can tape a toothbrush to outside of costume. This costume pairs up well with PACK OF GUM (page 60), CANDY BAR (page 61), or M&M (page 61).

PACK OF GUM

Cut two pieces of poster board or cardboard into long rectangles, about 15 × 28 inches. Use markers and poster paint to draw a facsimile of a pack of gum.

Wrap a piece of cardboard, 14 × 10 inches, in aluminum foil. (1) Cover all but the top 1½ inches of foil with white paper. Decorate the top 2–3 inches of paper to match the pack of gum. (2) Securely tape this piece of cardboard inside the front of the costume to simulate a stick of gum. (3) Repeat for the back piece of your costume.

Punch holes in the top of poster board pieces, and attach ribbon to hang over child's shoulders. If available, dab some peppermint extract on inside of costume so child will *smell* like a pack of gum!

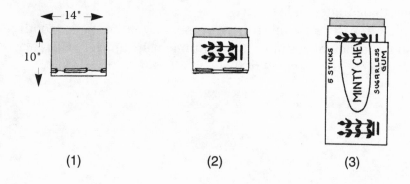

(1)   (2)   (3)

CANDY BAR

Follow instructions for PACK OF GUM, using favorite candy bar wrapper as guide. Wrap smaller pieces of cardboard in aluminum foil only, and tape to inside of costume at top and bottom (see illustration, page 60). Vanilla extract is a readily available "special effect."

M&M

Cut two circles, approximately 2–3 feet in diameter, from cardboard or colored poster board. If using cardboard, spray-paint in desired color and allow to dry. Using M&M wrapper as a model, copy M logo in center of each circle, and paint it white.

Punch two holes in tops of circles, about 7–9 inches apart, and attach ribbon for shoulder straps. Child may want to wear clothing and hat to match M&M color.

Activity to try:

- Put those M&M's to good use by adding them to your favorite cookie recipe or sprinkling them on brownie batter before baking.

back of flower mask

FLOWER

Cut poster board or cardboard about 24 inches square. Use colored poster board, or spray-paint both sides of cardboard with desired flower color.

Cut a hole in center of the poster board, so that child's face fits in hole. The fit should be snug but not too tight. Draw and cut out the desired flower shape around the hole. Petal cutting lines should end at least 2 inches from hole.

Use poster paint and markers to add details to petals.

Follow directions for How to Keep a Mask on Your Child's Head (page 122). If petals are too floppy, reinforce back of flower with Popsicle sticks taped across weak points (see above).

Child wears green or brown clothes, as "stem." If desired, cut out green paper leaf shapes, and tape or safety-pin to clothing.

Activities to try:

- Three or more children, dressed as different flowers, can trick-or-treat together as a "flower garden" or a "bouquet."

- A young flower can pretend to sprout, grow, and blossom in the morning sun. Child starts in curled-up position, then slowly stretches up. A little pretend watering is usually appreciated!

MASTERPIECE

Use a 2-foot square of cardboard or white poster board to make this simple costume.

Child uses poster paints, finger paints, markers, or collage materials to create his or her own artistic masterpiece. Frame artwork with wide strips of colored plastic tape, duct tape, or construction paper. Make a label for masterpiece, including artist and title, and attach to center bottom of frame.

Punch two holes in top of frame, centered and about 10 inches apart. Attach about 20 inches of ribbon, and hang around child's neck.

If desired and available, child may want to wear a beret and carry a paint brush.

Activities to try:

- Create a three-dimensional masterpiece by gluing dried beans, pasta shapes, colorful yarn, buttons, fabric scraps, and so on to poster board.

- You may want to copy a famous painting or drawing by a favorite artist. Look in art books for ideas.

BOARD GAME

Use two pieces of poster board or cardboard. Paint or draw a facsimile of your child's favorite board game box cover on one piece of poster board or cardboard.

On the second piece, paint or draw the game board itself. An especially simple game to duplicate is checkers. Paint a checkerboard pattern, and glue black and red painted milk bottle caps to the board as checkers.

More sophisticated game boards are a real challenge. If the board proves too complicated, draw a simplified version. Use aluminum foil to make models of metallic game pieces, and glue them to the board. Use construction paper, cardboard, or other materials to make flat or three-dimensional game pieces, cards, tokens, and so on, and glue these to the game board. If you have extra play money, glue some to the game board. You may wish to purchase inexpensive dice or plastic game pieces to glue down too.

Punch holes in top of board pieces, and attach ribbon as shoulder straps. Board game "cover" goes in front.

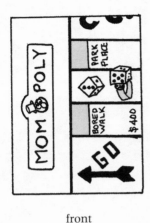

front

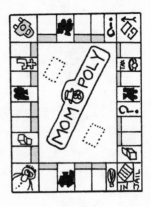

back

Activity to try:

- Throw a Game Party! Ask a few friends to dress up as their favorite games and bring the games along to play. Serve simple refreshments, and take turns playing everyone's favorite board games.

CARDBOARD BOX COSTUMES

box costumes are fun to build and make a big impression, partly because they're so *big*! They're great for indoor parties, since they're easy to remove for play and refreshments. For outdoor trick-or-treating, lots of warm clothing can be worn underneath, and reflective tape or foil can be incorporated into the costume design for safety.

The supplies needed for the following costumes are available at hardware or department stores, or around the house. They include:

- Spray paint, poster paint, or leftover latex paint
- Razor knife or heavy scissors for cutting cardboard
- Masking tape, colorful plastic tape ($\frac{3}{4}$-inch wide), duct tape, or colored cloth tape
- White paper, aluminum foil, construction paper
- Household odds and ends (bottle caps, cardboard tubes, egg cartons, plastic soda bottles, paper plates, etc.)
- Markers

SOME HINTS FOR BOX COSTUME CONSTRUCTION

- Box costumes are often large and bulky. BE EXTRA CAREFUL NEAR STAIRS!

- Think about the location of armholes. Depending on the fit of the box and the age of your child, you may want to put the armholes *in front* to protect against injury in case of a fall. If the box is close fitting, or if the costume is for an older child, armholes can be on the sides.

- Some costumes require the cardboard to be *scored*. *Scoring* means cutting through just the top layer of cardboard, so the cardboard bends along the score line. Do *not* cut all the way through!

- The CAR, LOCOMOTIVE, BULLDOZER, and FLYING SAUCER/UFO costumes are worn around the child's torso and hang from shoulder straps. Make the shoulder straps out of two long loops of wide ribbon. Install the straps by punching holes in the costume in front of and behind the hole for the child's torso. The two back holes should be closer together than the two front holes, to prevent the straps from slipping off the child's shoulders. Thread the ribbons into the holes, and tie each ribbon to form a big loop, as shown in the costume illustrations. Adjust the strap length to fit your child.

CANDY MACHINE

(This costume is a big hit at parties!)

Remove top flaps from a large box. Turn the box over, and cut a hole for child's head. Box will rest on child's shoulders. Cut arm-holes, if desired.

Cover the outside of the box with paint or paper to resemble a vending machine. Any color will do.

Have child wear box, and figure out appropriate spot for "Candy Dispenser Slot." It should be within child's easy reach from inside the box. With child *out* of box, cut a dispenser slot about 3 × 4 inches. If desired, you can also cut a money slot, taping a small plastic bag over opening on inside of box, to catch coins.

Use paint or markers to decorate the outside of the box to look like a candy vending machine. Be sure to add labels, arrows, and directions so people know how to operate the machine. You may also want to glue sample candies to the sides of the machine for decoration.

At the time of the party, child stands inside box, equipped with a bag of inexpensive candies. When a "customer" inserts a penny (or homemade paper coin), child drops a piece of candy out the dispenser slot. (You may want to have a supply of pennies available to guests.)

Variations:

- If dispenser slot ends up being too low, tape a paper towel tube above the slot, and child can drop candy down tube.

- If desired, you can make this a FREE CANDY MACHINE. Omit the money slot, and attach a "push button" instead. Label the machine and button accordingly.

- For the health-conscious, try a PEANUT VENDING MACHINE, dispensing peanuts in the shell.

- For those on a diet, try a FORTUNE TELLING MACHINE, dispensing fortunes written on slips of paper.

ROBOT

Find a medium- to large-size box that is fairly close-fitting on your child. Remove the top flaps, turn the box over, and cut holes for child's head and arms. (1)

Cut a door, about 6 × 6 inches, in upper chest area, as shown. (2) From inside of box, place a piece of cardboard over door opening and tape in place. This will be the robot's main circuit board. (3) If desired, other, smaller doors and circuit boards can be located on the robot body, to "control" other robotic functions.

(1)

(2)

(3)

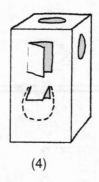

(4)

If costume is for Halloween, cut another door, about 3 × 5 inches, below the main circuit board. This door should open upwards. (4) From inside of box, use duct tape to *securely* attach a sturdy plastic bag around slot, to collect candy. Choose a bag that won't hang below bottom of box.

Paint the box silver or gray. Be sure to paint the insides of the doors and circuit boards.

When paint is dry, outfit your robot with all the latest in robotic technology. Glue colored wires onto circuit board, or substitute colored yarn or pipe cleaners. Use wire, pipe cleaners, or a purchased knob to make a door handle. (5)

Visit a hardware store for inexpensive electrical supplies to glue to the outside of your robot. Or draw dials, buttons, and switches

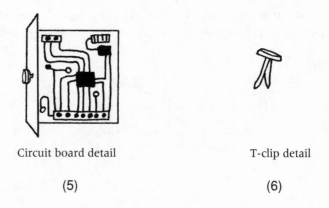

Circuit board detail

(5)

T-clip detail

(6)

on paper, and glue or tape them to the robot body. Attach some dials with T-clips so they can turn. (6)

Plastic soda bottles are a good source for colored or clear plastic. Cut dome shapes, and attach them to the robot body with silver duct tape. For an interesting effect, line the inside of a plastic dome with aluminum foil before attaching to robot.

Other robot attachments found around the home might include sections of egg cartons or rectangular pieces cut from a mesh onion bag. Fasten these items to the robot with tape, and finish with spray paint.

If you have cut a candy slot, label clearly, "Insert Candy Here."

If available, child can wear an oversize gray or black sweatshirt or jacket, large gloves, and heavy boots.

Activities to try:

• Make a CARDBOARD BOX ROBOT HELMET. Find or make a small, close-fitting box to fit your child's head. Remove the top flaps, and cut a space for child's face, as shown. Cut a few small holes in sides of box, so child can hear easily. See costume illustration, page 71.

  Paint helmet silver or gray. Attach long pipe cleaners for radio antennae, and glue on dials, buttons, and wires similar to those used on robot body.

• For other activities, see PAPER BAG ROBOT (page 36).

BANK SAFE

Remove top flaps from a large- or medium-size square box. Turn the box over, and cut holes for child's head and arms.

Paint the box gray. When paint is dry, draw a door and hinges with black marker or poster paint. Write a bank company logo on the sides of the safe. (1)

Use a 7-ounce paper cup and a small (7-inch) paper plate to make a lock mechanism. Cut a hole in the center of the plate, slightly larger than the bottom of the paper cup. (2)

Cut off the top 1½ inches of the paper cup. (3)

Measure 1 inch from the bottom of the cup, and cut slits from the top to that point. Bend the resulting tabs out, as shown. (4)

Cover the bottom section of the cup with aluminum foil, and slide it through the hole in the plate so that it comes out the *bottom* of the plate. (5) Fit should be snug enough to hold aluminum foil and cup in place. If not, add a little tape.

Use black marker to draw a pointer on the aluminum foil, and lines and numbers on the plate bottom, as shown. (6) Glue or tape the lock mechanism to the door of the safe. Draw a bank logo, company name, and decorations on the safe door. Cut a simple handle out of cardboard, paint it black, and glue it to the door.

If desired, cut a few slits along door outline, and slide play money (purchased or homemade) partway into safe. Tape in place on inside of box.

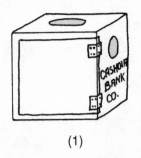

(1)

(2)

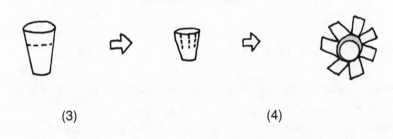

(3)

(4)

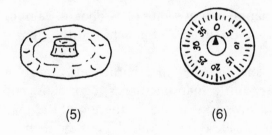

(5)

(6)

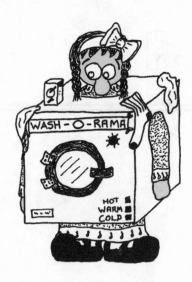

WASHING MACHINE

Remove top flaps from a large, square box. Turn the box over, and cut holes for child's head and arms.

Paint the box white, or cover with white paper. Using a dinner plate as a guide, trace a large circle (about 10 inches in diameter) in the center of one of the box sides. This will be the washing machine door. Cut out the circle, and, working inside the box, stretch one thickness of a clear plastic bag across the opening. Tape securely on the inside of the box.

Use markers or paint to add a gray, black, or silver border around the door. Draw two large hinges on the left side of the door, and make a simple handle out of scraps of cardboard. Paint or color the handle gray, black, or silver, and attach it to the right side of the door.

Use markers, construction paper, bottle caps, and so on to decorate the washer with a manufacturer's logo, dials, and buttons. Staple or tape a few socks or rags to the top of the machine, and hang a few more inside the machine door, to be seen through the window. Finally, glue a small, empty detergent box (from Laundromat) to the top of the washing machine.

DINNER TABLE

Remove top flaps from a large box. Turn the box over, and paint the sides with any dark color. When paint is dry, cover the unpainted portion and the box sides with an inexpensive paper tablecloth. Use scissors and markers to add fringe, a scalloped edge, a checkered pattern, or whatever you like. Glue or tape the tablecloth securely in place.

Cut a hole for the child's head to fit through. The box will rest on child's shoulders. If box is smallish, cut armholes.

Glue on paper and plastic place settings, cups, and napkins. Add a small teapot or sugar bowl from a plastic tea set, if desired. For a final touch, child can wear a real or paper lampshade for a hat.

Variations:

- For an especially elegant look, try painting place settings with gold spray paint. Child's "centerpiece" headgear can be a light-weight candlestick or a bouquet of flowers.

JUICE BOX

Remove top flaps from a medium-size box. Turn the box over, and cut holes for child's head and arms. Cover entire surface of box with either paper or paint, and decorate it to resemble the packaging of your child's favorite boxed drink.

Use a cardboard tube from a roll of paper towels or gift wrap to make a straw. Cover the tube with white paper or paint. Draw or paint a red spiral around the tube, or use red plastic tape. Cut a hole, the diameter of the cardboard tube, in the top of the juice box near a front corner. Insert the "straw" in the hole, and secure with tape on the inside of the box.

BASKETBALL HOOP

Find a box that is wide but not very deep. Remove the top flaps, turn the box over, and cut a hole for child's head, as shown. (1)

Paint the box white, or cover it with white paper.

Pull a wire clothes hanger into a circle shape, and straighten out the handle as shown on page 80. (2) Poke the handle through the box, as shown in Figure 3. Working inside the box, wrap pieces of

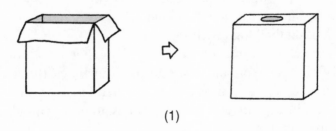

(1)

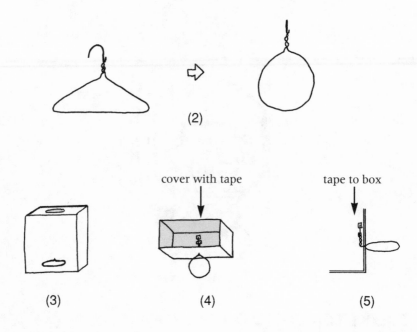

(2)

cover with tape

tape to box

(3)   (4)   (5)

duct tape around the sharp ends of the wire hanger, to protect child from getting scratched. (4)

Bend the hanger handle up inside the box, and tape securely to the inside with duct tape. (5)

Cut armholes in front of box so that child can rebound light-weight sponge balls or candy. (6)

Use ¾-inch red plastic tape (available in hardware stores) to add backboard trim. (6) The curved line at the top of the backboard can be achieved by cutting nicks in the tape as you lay it down. (7) Fill in the nicks later, with slivers of tape.

Draw a basketball logo with markers.

If desired, you can make a fabric net from cheesecloth or a similar gauzy material. To make a simple and quick net, though, use a sturdy plastic bag. A white plastic department store bag works well. Turn it inside out, and draw a net design on it with black permanent marker. (8)

Fit the bag inside the wire hanger frame, and fold the top of the bag over the hanger. Tape securely with duct tape. If child will be collecting candy in basket, make extra sure that bag is sturdy and well taped.

Activity to try:

- Child can carry a lightweight sponge ball for a traveling basketball game. Be sure armholes are positioned so that ball is easy for child to retrieve, rebound, and toss back to friends.

(6)   (7)   (8)

TELEVISION SET

Remove the top flaps from a medium-size box. Turn the box over, and either cover it with brown paper or paint it to give it a "wood" finish. Or, for a futuristic look, cover the box with aluminum foil. (This is highly visible when trick-or-treating in the dark.)

Box will rest on child's head. Cut a television screen shape out of one side. Depending on size of box, you may want to cut arm-holes. Cover milk or soda bottle caps with construction paper, aluminum foil, or paint, and attach them to television set with tape or glue. Use permanent marker to label these knobs: On, Off, Channel, and so on.

If desired, make a remote control for child to carry. Use either a small, oblong box or two to three rectangular pieces of cardboard taped together. Cover with paper, and decorate with markers.

Activities to try:

- Your child can be a one-person television show: announcer, actor, and commercials all rolled into one funny performance. If the box is big enough, two children can fit in one screen for a talk show, comedy routine, or musical.

- Play a silly channel cruising game. One person "switches channels" with the remote control as the child in the television changes "shows." Go from singing a song to forecasting the weather to acting out a western to hosting a talk show to learning the alphabet to reporting the news—all in five minutes!

GIFT BOX

This costume can be put together in minutes. Remove the top flaps from a large- or medium-size box. Cover the outside of the box with gift wrap. (An inexpensive alternative to gift wrap is leftovers from prepasted wallpaper. Just apply as you would to walls, except this is much easier!) Cut holes for child's head and arms.

Tape wide strips of brightly colored construction paper around the box to resemble a ribbon. Add an oversize gift tag. Child wears huge bow on head that matches the ribbon color.

CAR

Find a sturdy rectangular box. Carefully remove top flaps to use later. Turn box over, and cut a square hole for child's torso. (1)

Trim the bottom box edge on each side to make a "wheel base," as shown. (2)

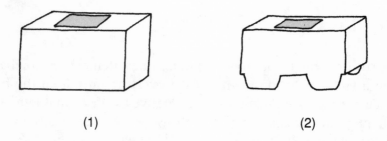

(1)   (2)

From the top flaps, or extra pieces of cardboard, cut the following pieces, as illustrated in Figure 3:

- two sets of side windows
- windshield

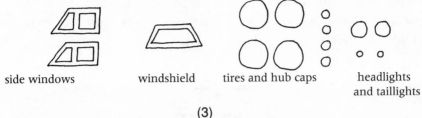

side windows   windshield   tires and hub caps   headlights
                                                                      and taillights

(3)

- four circles to cover wheel bases, as tires; four smaller circles to serve as hubcaps
- two circles, 3 inches in diameter, for headlights
- two smaller circles for taillights

Use heavy tape and/or glue to attach side windows and windshield. (4)

Paint car whatever color child chooses. Paint four tire circles black. Paint headlight circles bright yellow and taillight circles red. Allow paint to dry.

Use paint or markers to draw doors, handles, trunk, and car logo. (5)

Glue or tape tires to wheel bases. Cover hubcap circles with aluminum foil, and attach to tires with loops of heavy tape. (5)

Cover a cardboard tube from bathroom tissue with aluminum foil, and attach to back of car as exhaust pipe. (5)

Make license plates out of construction paper, using your state's colors, if possible. Attach to front and back of car. (5)

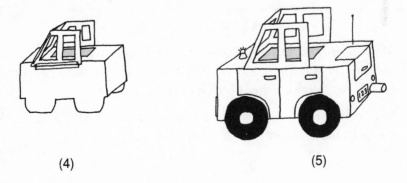

(4)   (5)

Cardboard Box Costumes **85**

Punch holes in front of and behind space for child's torso, and attach wide ribbon straps, as shown in Figure 6. (See SOME HINTS FOR BOX COSTUME CONSTRUCTION, page 68.) Costume hangs from child's shoulders.

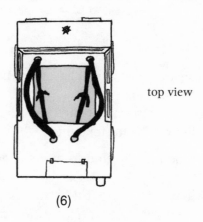

top view

(6)

Variations:

- Extra trim for car: pipe cleaner radio antenna; plastic wrap taped over windows to simulate glass; inexpensive bicycle horn attached to side of car; hood ornament of child's choosing; grille and bumpers made from cardboard covered with aluminum foil.

- Make a sporty-looking race car by painting the car bright colors and adding a large number on each side. Back tires should be oversize.

Activities to try:

- Make a simple map of your house, yard, or neighborhood. Mark a route on the map, and have "car" follow it. When child runs out of gas, offer a drink of milk or juice!

- Teach child hand signals to use when turning or stopping. These come in handy later on, for bicycle safety.

LOCOMOTIVE

Find a sturdy rectangular box. Carefully remove top flaps to use later. Turn box over, and cut a square hole for child's torso. This hole should be toward the back of the box. (1)

Trim the bottom box edge on each side to make a "wheel base" for two large and two small wheels. (2)

Trim the back of the box, as shown in Figure 3, and cut the front of the box to resemble a locomotive's grille or "cowcatcher." (3)

Make two 2-inch cuts in top of box, score cardboard on inside, and bend the cardboard up to form a control panel. Tape in place on both sides of bend. (4)

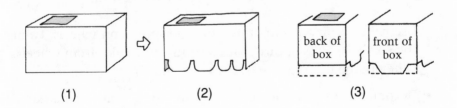

(1)   (2)   (3)

From the top flaps, and/or extra pieces of cardboard, cut the following pieces, as illustrated in Figure 5:

- two sets of side windows
- one rear window
- eight circles to cover wheel bases: four large and four small
- six long, thin pieces, about $\frac{1}{2} \times 6$ inches, for wheel trim
- one circle, 3 inches in diameter, for headlight

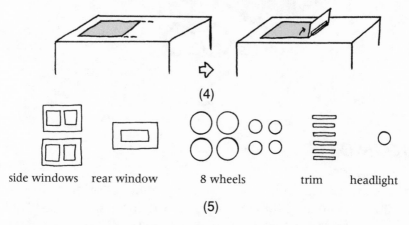

(4)

side windows   rear window   8 wheels   trim   headlight

(5)

Use heavy tape and/or glue to attach the windows and wheels, as shown. (6) Bend cowcatcher forward slightly. (6)

★ *Note:* If wheels will be a different color than body of train, paint them first and attach them after all paint has dried.

Cut a cardboard tube from paper towels or bathroom tissue about 2–3 inches long. Attach to top of engine. (6)

Paint entire locomotive, inside and out, black, silver, or whatever color child chooses. Allow paint to dry, then add trim:

- Use paint or markers to draw rims and spokes on wheels. Paint the six thin pieces of cardboard a contrasting color from wheels. Glue or tape from hub to hub, as shown. (7)

- Decorate sides and back of locomotive with paint or markers. Draw railroad company name, designs, and vertical lines on cowcatcher, as illustrated. (7)

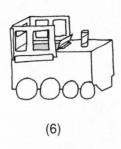

(6)

Boxy Express

(7)

- Add paper dials and switches to control panel, if desired.

- Paint the 3-inch cardboard circle bright yellow. Attach to front of locomotive as headlight. (7)

   Punch holes in front of and behind space for child's torso, and attach wide ribbon straps, as shown in Figure 8. (See SOME HINTS FOR BOX COSTUME CONSTRUCTION, page 68.) Costume hangs from child's shoulders.

   Child wears an engineer's cap, if available, or a baseball cap. Overalls, heavy gloves, and a red kerchief around neck complete the look.

Activities to try:

- Dragging a chair on a plush carpet creates an instant "track" for a locomotive to follow.

- Young engineers can double as conductors, calling out, "All aboard!," "Tickets, please!," and "Next stop, Danny's bedroom!" Passengers carry homemade tickets and follow the engine in a line.

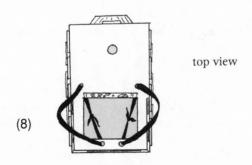

top view

(8)

Cardboard Box Costumes 89

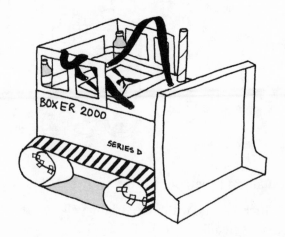

BULLDOZER

You will need two boxes and a paper towel tube to make this powerful costume. Find a sturdy rectangular box and a second, similar-size box for extra cardboard supply.

Trim the first box, as shown, so that it is about 12 inches high. (1) Turn box over, and cut a square hole for child's torso. This hole should be toward the back of the box. (2)

Make two 2-inch cuts in top of box, as illustrated in Figure 3. Score cardboard from inside, and bend the flap up to form a control panel. Tape in place on both sides of bend. (4)

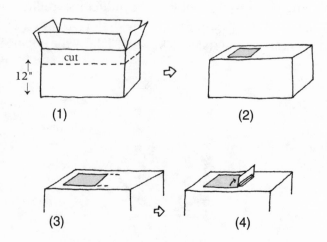

Cut a bulldozer blade from the bottom of the second box, as shown in Figure 5.

From the remaining cardboard, cut the following pieces, as illustrated in Figure 6:

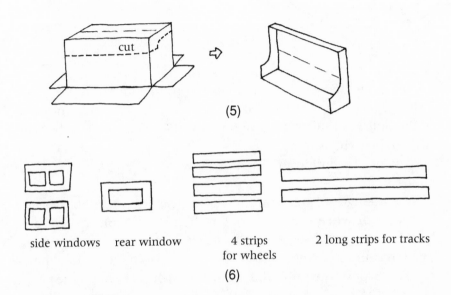

(5)

side windows   rear window   4 strips   2 long strips for tracks
                                    for wheels
(6)

- two sets of side windows

- one rear window

- four strips 24 × 4 inches for wheels

- two very long strips for tracks, approximately 4 × 60 inches (you should figure this measurement after you have attached the bulldozer wheels). If long cardboard is unavailable, you can substitute brown paper grocery bags, cut and folded to proper size and length.

To make the bulldozer's wheels, bend the 24-inch strips into four circles and tape securely.

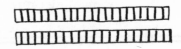

(7)   (8)

Use heavy tape and/or glue to attach the windows, wheels, and bulldozer blade to box, as shown. (7) Cut a hole toward the front of the bulldozer just big enough to insert a paper towel tube. This will be the exhaust pipe. (7)

Paint entire bulldozer bright yellow or whatever color child chooses.

To find length of track pieces, use a measuring tape to measure around *both* wheels on each side of bulldozer. From either cardboard or brown paper grocery bags, cut two strips, 4 inches wide, by determined length (approximately 60 inches). Use black marker or poster paint to draw track on strips, as shown. (8) Tape and/or glue strips in place around wheels. See costume illustration, page 90.

Use paint or markers to decorate sides and back of bulldozer with company name and logo.

If desired, add paper dials and switches to control panel.

Attach wide ribbon straps as shown, so costume hangs from child's shoulders. (See SOME HINTS FOR BOX COSTUME CONSTRUCTION, page 68.)

If bulldozer sags forward, you need to balance the costume. Partially fill two small plastic soda bottles with water, and position one in each back corner of the bulldozer cab. When balance is corrected, secure bottles in corners with duct tape. See costume illustration.

Child wears hard hat, if available, sweatshirt, jeans, work boots, and gloves.

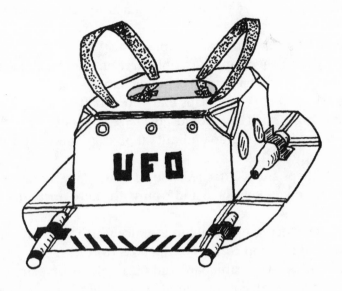

FLYING SAUCER/UFO

This unusual costume is very big and very flashy!

Find a medium to large cube-shaped box. Carefully remove the top flaps to use later. (1) You may want to have a second box handy for extra cardboard.

Cut 8–12 inches down at each corner, as shown. (2) The longer the cuts at this point, the larger the costume will be.

Use a razor knife to lightly *score* the inside of the box from

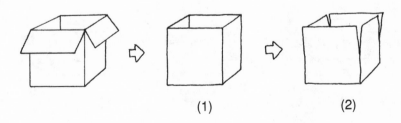

(1)   (2)

corner to corner, at the cuts. (See page 68 for an explanation of scoring.) (3)

Bend each side out at score line. (4)

Turn the box over, and cut a hole large enough for child's torso. (5) The costume will hang from shoulder straps, around child's middle.

Attach each of the top flaps that you cut off earlier at a corner, as shown. (6) Top flaps should go *under* box flaps and should be attached with both glue and duct tape (top and bottom) to make them really secure.

When flaps are all attached, use scissors or a razor knife to round the outer edge. Reinforce and trim with more duct tape, if necessary. (7)

This next step is optional but is a nice touch. Use a razor knife to cut off the four top corners of the box. (8) Cover the resulting triangular holes with cardboard and duct tape. (9) If extra cardboard is unavailable, an interesting effect can be obtained by covering the holes with sturdy plastic wrap and securing the edges with duct tape.

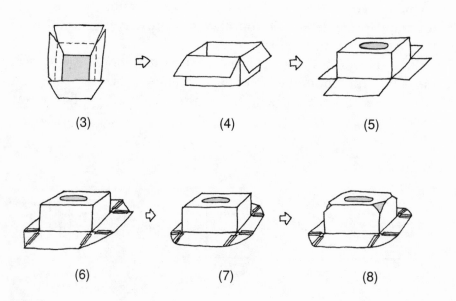

(3)   (4)   (5)

(6)   (7)   (8)

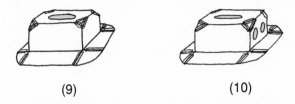

(9)   (10)

If desired, cut a few portholes in the sides of the box, and cover these from inside the box with sturdy plastic wrap. Tape plastic in place with duct tape. (10)

Take the UFO outdoors, and spray-paint all surfaces (*including* plastic wrap) silver. It is not necessary to paint the underside of the UFO. Allow paint to dry thoroughly.

Your child will have his or her own ideas about how to decorate the flying saucer. Here are some suggestions, as shown in the costume illustration, page 93:

- Use red plastic tape to add trim and "UFO" in large letters on the front.

- Cover two paper towel tubes with aluminum foil. Trim the front end of each tube with red tape. Use duct tape to secure these "laser guns" to the front of the flying saucer.

- Tape or glue bright yellow or red milk bottle caps to upper edge of UFO, as lights.

- Spray-paint plastic soda bottles silver, gold, or black, and attach them to the body of the flying saucer as "warp engines."

- Attach a small flashlight or "glow-in-the-dark stickers" to body of UFO.

Finally, attach wide ribbon straps as shown, so costume hangs from child's shoulders (see SOME HINTS FOR BOX COSTUME CONSTRUC-TION, page 68).

For that perfect, final touch, child can wear green face makeup, swim or ski goggles, and a helmet. A bicycle helmet covered with aluminum foil works fine.

FABRIC COSTUMES

a little sewing can go a long way. The following instructions for Circle Costumes, Tunics and Vests, and Capes require little sewing experience and only the most basic skills. A sewing machine is fast but certainly not necessary.

Felt is one of the easiest fabrics to work with. It comes in various weights and bright colors, cuts easily, and requires no hemming. For more of a challenge, look for unusual fabrics in your store's remnant piles. Silky and shiny fabrics make wonderful capes. Most polyester knits have edges that won't unravel, making hemming optional. Specialty fabrics such as vinyl cloth, decorative lace, and fake furs will lend themselves to lots of creative ideas.

You can also turn unwanted household items into fabulous costumes. Old drapes, tablecloths, sheets, or fabric shower curtains can make regal-looking capes and tunics. Filmy curtains are perfect for angel wings or a fairy's Circle Costume.

The patterns that follow are very simple. If, however, you are not quite sure how to fit the illustrations to your child, try making a pattern out of newspaper first. A common mistake is to make the costume too tight. Allow for plenty of room, keeping in mind that it's easy to trim a too-large costume, whereas adding fabric can be tricky.

BASIC STITCHES AND SEWING TERMS

Basting Stitch

A large running stitch. Use to hold
fabric in place or to gather fabric.

Running Stitch

For simple hemming and seams.

Overcast Stitch

Also for hemming, and for attaching ears, antennae, and so on to
costumes.

Topstitch

A running stitch, often in contrasting color thread, sewn on outside of costume, to add trim or color, or to hold fabric in place.

Selvage

The edge or sides of fabric
woven so as not to unravel.

Interfacing

A specialty fabric sewn to the
wrong side of some fabrics to
stiffen them.

TWELVE-STITCH CIRCLE COSTUME

★ *Note:* This is a fast and easy "winged" costume especially suited for young children. It fits nicely over play clothes for indoor play or over snowsuits for outdoor trick-or-treating in chilly weather.

While child stands with arms outstretched, measure wrist to wrist. (1)

Fold fabric in half, and cut half circle with folded diameter equal to wrist-to-wrist measurement. (2) If fabric is thin, you may want to fold in quarters to make cutting a circle easier. If you plan to hem fabric edges, make circle a bit larger all around.

Find center point on folded edge. Cut a shallow slit for child's head to poke through. (3) *Be careful not to make the slit too large. Start small and enlarge, if necessary.* Hem edges, if desired.

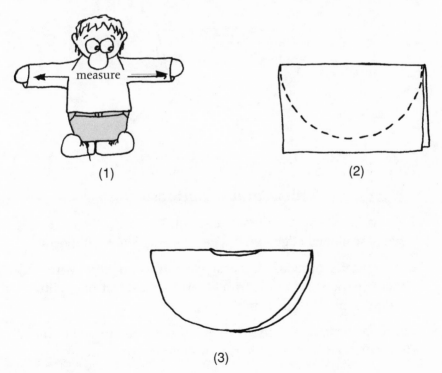

(1)

(2)

(3)

Have child try on costume with arms outstretched. Adjust the length, if necessary, then pin loosely under child's arms, as shown. (4) Use yarn to make six large basting stitches under each arm, to form sleeves. (5)

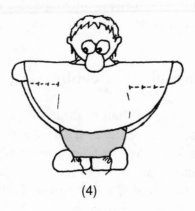

(4)

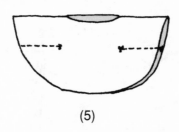

(5)

Ideas and variations:

- Use scissors to trim the outside edge of the CIRCLE COSTUME. Cut fringe, a scalloped edge, or a ragged edge, as shown opposite.

- Add decorations the fast and easy way: draw on fabric with permanent markers; glue on trim (fabric scraps, buttons, glitter); try colorful plastic tape trim.

- A very short version of the CIRCLE COSTUME can be used to make wide, round collars for a Pilgrim or Egyptian costume.

CIRCLE BUTTERFLY

Use any colorful fabric to make a CIRCLE COSTUME. You may want to cut gently scalloped outside edges, although this is not necessary.

Decorate front and back of "wings" with ovals, circles, and other shapes cut from contrasting fabric scraps. Attach with stitches or glue.

Use permanent marker to draw a simple outline of the butterfly's body, as shown.

To make antennae, use an overcast stitch to attach black pipe cleaners to the sides of a brightly colored knit hat. Slightly bend the ends outward, as illustrated above. Or, try ANTENNAE, page 144.

★ *Note:* See also WIRE-WING BUTTERFLY (page 16).

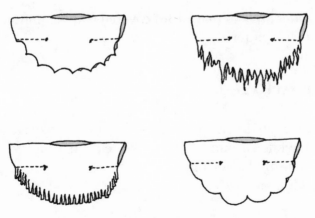

Activity to try:

- Visit your library to find pictures of different butterflies. Your child can choose a particular butterfly to copy. Look for fabric colors to match your butterfly's wings.

CIRCLE FAIRY

Make a CIRCLE COSTUME from sheer fabric. Recycled sheer curtains work well. Sheer fabrics with a floral pattern are especially nice. If desired, decorate with glue and glitter.

Child wears costume over light-colored leotard and tights or play clothes.

Make ANTENNAE (page 144), or, for a royal look, make a CROWN (pages 126–27).

Child carries a WAND (page 136) covered with aluminum foil and decorated with glitter.

CIRCLE ANGEL

Use opaque white fabric to make a CIRCLE COSTUME (page 99). Trim edges with white glue and glitter, or leave plain. Child wears white tights or pants under costume.

Make HALO (page 132).

CIRCLE GHOST

Make a CIRCLE COSTUME from opaque, white fabric. An old sheet is perfect. Cut more of an oval shape for this costume, making the front and back slightly longer than the sides. Leave the edges ragged.

Child wears white face makeup, with dark circles around eyes.

TUNICS AND VESTS

NO-SEW TUNIC

Avoid hemming edges by choosing a fabric that doesn't fray: felt, polyester knit, vinyl cloth, suede cloth, and so on.

After measuring child for width and length, fold fabric in half, and cut shape as shown on page 104. Cut short slit at *front* of neckline only.

Variations for neckline shape and bottom edge trim are detailed in the illustration on page 105 and in individual costume instructions.

Cut a belt out of fabric, or use a purchased belt to hold tunic closed. If using vinyl cloth, you can hold the tunic sides closed with colorful plastic tape. This tape can also be used for trim. (See SUPERHEROES, page 118.)

NO SEW TUNIC

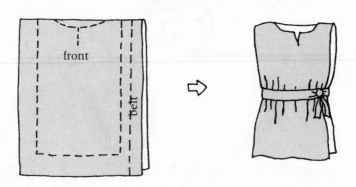

EASY-SEW TUNIC

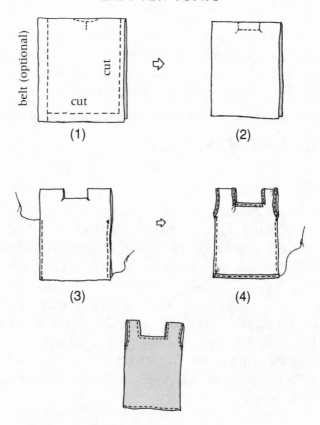

EASY-SEW TUNIC

After measuring child for width and length, fold fabric in half, and cut shape as shown in Figure 1. Be sure to allow extra width for seams and hems.

Decide on style of neckline, as indicated in costume directions or illustration (below), and cut. (2) Remember to cut neckline *small,* allowing for hem.

Turn tunic wrong side out, and sew side seams as shown, leaving large armholes. (3)

At neckline and armholes, fold fabric over, and sew to form a finished edge. (4)

Trim bottom edge as indicated in costume instructions or illustration below. Fold raw edges under and hem. (4)

If desired, cut a belt out of fabric, or use a purchased belt.

TUNIC TRIM

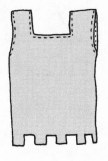

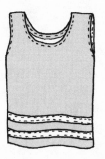

QUICKIE VEST

Use PAPER BAG NATIVE AMERICAN VEST (page 38) as a pattern. (1)

To avoid sewing, choose a nonfraying fabric. Or, depending on the costume, a rustic, frayed look may be just right. (Denim edges fray nicely when laundered.) If you plan to hem edges, be sure to allow for extra fabric.

If desired, sew buttons on either side of front, and use yarn to close. (2) Or sew a button on one side and cut a small buttonhole on the opposite side.

Variation:

•Make a full-length vest, as shown below. Close with Velcro tabs. (3)

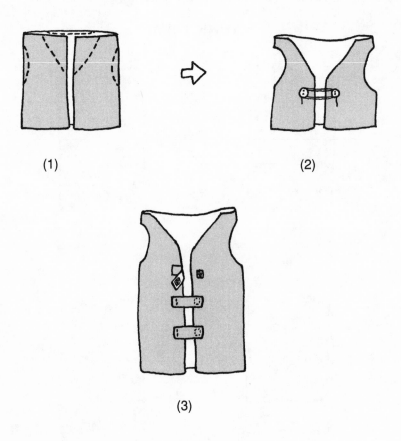

(1)   (2)

(3)

WIRE-WING FAIRY

Child wears light-colored leotard and tights, a midlength EASY-SEW TUNIC (page 105), WIRE WINGS (page 148), and either ANTENNAE (page 144) or a CROWN (pages 126–27).

Use a lightweight, sheer fabric to make the tunic and wings, leaving tunic bottom and outside wing edges a bit ragged, as shown. Decorate with white glue and glitter, or leave plain if fabric has a pattern.

If available, use shiny silver pipe cleaners for ANTENNAE (page 144) or PIPE CLEANER CROWN (page 127).

Child carries WAND (page 136).

WIRE-WING ANGEL

Child wears white clothing under a long, white, EASY-SEW TUNIC (page 105). Add WIRE WINGS (page 148) and a HALO (page 132).

Use a medium-weight, flowing, white fabric to make the tunic and white panty hose or sheer, white fabric to make the wings. Leave extra fabric hanging from outside edges of wings, as shown. Decorate wings with glue and glitter, or leave plain.

ROBIN HOOD

Use either green or brown fabric (felt, knits, suede cloth) to make a NO-SEW TUNIC (page 103) or an EASY-SEW TUNIC (page 105) secured at waist with purchased or fabric belt. If desired, cut the bottom of the tunic into a blocked edge, as shown. Child wears tunic over a brown, green, or white turtleneck or T-shirt, and either brown or green pants or tights.

Make an ADVENTURER'S HAT (page 130) out of green fabric.

Child can carry a BOW AND ARROWS (page 155) and a QUIVER (page 155).

PETER PAN

Make a NO-SEW TUNIC (page 103) or an EASY-SEW TUNIC (page 105) out of green fabric (felt, knits, suede cloth). Secure at waist with fabric belt. The bottom of the tunic should have ragged edges, as shown. Child wears tunic over a white turtleneck or T-shirt, and green tights.

Make an ADVENTURER'S HAT (page 130) out of green fabric.

Tuck a short DAGGER (page 156) into belt.

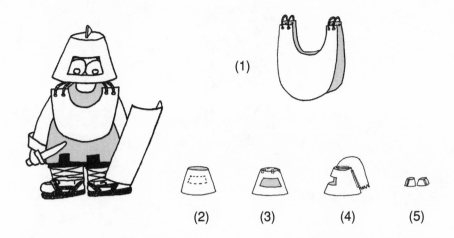

(1)

(2)   (3)   (4)   (5)

GLADIATOR

Cut two pieces of silver or gold poster board (available in stationery stores) into the breastplate shape, as shown above. (1)
Make sure that shoulder measurement matches child's shoulders,
and that armor extends to waist level or a little below. Punch two
holes at the top of each shoulder section, and attach ribbon or cord
to make sandwich board.

Use the remaining pieces of poster board to make a GLADIATOR
HELMET. Curve a long piece around child's head, forming a gentle
cone shape, open at the top. (2) Tape securely with silver duct tape
or colorful cloth tape. Make pencil markings on front of helmet to
show where child's eyes are. (2)

Remove helmet and cut rectangular window for child's eyes. (3)

Cut a circle to fit on top of helmet. Tape in place. (3)

Cut a trim piece to serve as the helmet's plume, as shown in Figure 4. Tape in place.

Use poster board scraps to make wristbands. (5)

Child wears EASY-SEW TUNIC (page 105), sandals, and, if desired,
can wrap lower legs in crisscrossed cord, brown yarn, or narrow ribbon.

Gladiator weaponry includes a short SWORD (page 156) and a
large, rectangular SHIELD (page 159).

CAVE DWELLER

Find fake fur in your fabric store to make this easy, funny, prehistoric costume.

Make a fake fur No-Sew Tunic (page 103) with uneven, ragged edges. Child wears tunic over tank top and shorts. Use a thin strip of fake fur to hold tunic closed.

If costume is to be worn indoors, child can go barefoot. Make sure child's hair is messy and tangled. Short hair may require mousse or gel. If desired, child can get that I-live-in-a-cave look by smudging a bit of Burnt Cork Dirt (page 164) on arms, legs, and face.

An easy prop to carry is a wheel cut out of brown corrugated cardboard. Smart cave dwellers carry round wheels, whereas unenlightened cave dwellers carry square wheels.

Activities to try:

- Make an indoor cave. Try draping a blanket over a card table or other medium-size table. Or set sofa cushions on their sides for walls, and cover the construction with a blanket. Stock the cave with supplies for prehistoric activities such as drawing, snacking, or napping.

- Some cave people may want to communicate using sign language rather than speaking.

- An adult or older child could take the cave dweller on a tour of the house, carefully explaining all the modern conveniences and their uses!

CAPES AND APRONS

Brightly colored felt is easy to work with and requires no hemming. Shiny, silky capes take more work, but they feel, look, and sound "swishier." You and your child can decide which look you want. The illustration on page 112 shows some simple ways to trim your cape.

No-Sew Cape, Easy-Sew Cape, and Basic Cape patterns and instructions can all be used to make Aprons. Simply adjust the length of the fabric, and make sure the ties are long enough to fit around child's waist.

NO-SEW CAPE

Fabric should be at least 36 inches wide. Measure child for width and length of cape, making a newspaper pattern, if desired. Cut fabric as shown, forming 1½-inch-wide ties and leaving 6–8 inches of uncut fabric behind child's neck. Use selvage edges as sides of cape to avoid having to hem.

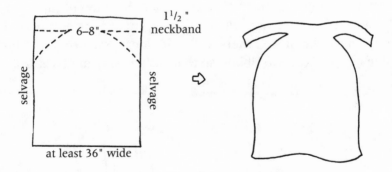

CAPE TRIM

EASY-SEW CAPE

Fabric should be at least 36 inches wide. Use selvage edges as sides of cape, to avoid having to hem. Hem bottom of cape. Fold over top edge about 1½ inches and sew, forming a tube at top of cape. (1)

Thread long, 1-inch-wide ribbon through tube as a tie. Have child try on cape and adjust gathers to fit shoulders. Safety-pin or stitch outside edges of cape to ribbon so that gathers stay in place. (2)

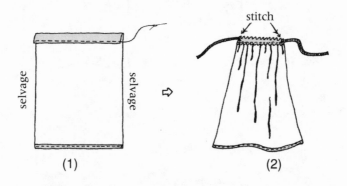

BASIC CAPE

This pattern works best with silky or lightweight fabrics. You will need about 1 yard of fabric, 36–45 inches wide. Use selvage edges as sides of cape, to avoid having to hem.

To make the neckband, cut a 3-inch strip of fabric from the top edge of cape. (1) Fold edges of strip over $\frac{3}{8}$ inch and iron. (2) Fold strip in half the long way and iron. (3)

Hem bottom edge of cape. Baste along top edge. (4)

Gather cape to width that matches child's shoulders (approximately 12–16 inches). (5)

Center the gathered edge of cape inside the folded neckband strip. Pin in place, and sew. (6)

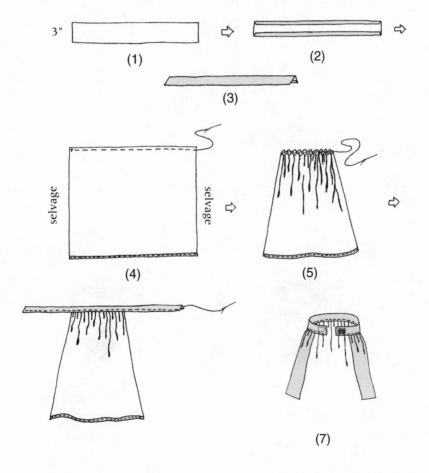

Variation:

• If you prefer a Velcro neck closure, trim neckband so that strips overlap 1–2 inches around child's neck. Sew Velcro tabs to ends of strips, as shown on page 113. (7) Velcro closures are especially recommended for very young children.

SWEATSHIRT CAPE

A simple cape can be sewn directly to a sweatshirt. Hem top and bottom edges of fabric, but baste and gather only the outer thirds of the top edge. (1) Try to use selvage edges as sides of cape, to avoid having to hem sides.

Use overcast stitch to attach these gathered sections to sweatshirt shoulders, leaving center section loose and sagging slightly. (2)

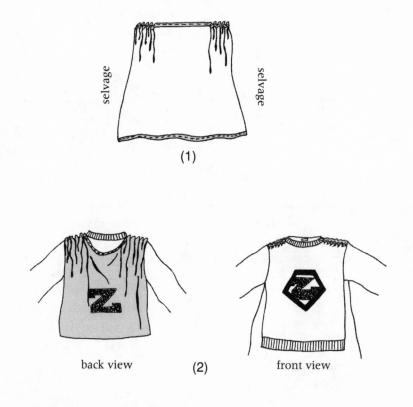

selvage   selvage

(1)

back view   (2)   front view

WITCH

Make a long EASY-SEW TUNIC (page 105) out of black fabric. Tie at waist with ragged, black sash belt. Bottom edges of tunic should be ragged. Child wears tunic over black, long-sleeved shirt or leotard.

Make a medium-length, black CAPE (pages 111–14), cutting bottom edges to be very ragged.

Child wears green face makeup and messy hair. A YARN WIG (page 138), worn under a purchased witch's hat or a black kerchief, looks very convincing.

Witches carry straw brooms for convenient transportation.

Variation:

- This costume can easily be modified for a SORCERER or SORCERESS. Make both the TUNIC and CAPE full-length, with smooth edges rather than ragged. Decorate the cape with felt cutouts of crescent moons and stars.

  If desired, make a tall CONE HAT (page 125), and decorate it with paper moons and stars.

  Sorcerers carry MAGICIAN'S WAND (page 136) and thick books of magic spells and recipes.

Activity to try:

- Cook up a WITCH'S BREW of hot, spiced apple cider. Combine 1 quart of cider with ½ teaspoon cinnamon, ½ teaspoon whole cloves, ⅛ teaspoon allspice, and a pinch of ginger. Bring to a boil, stir in ⅛ cup of brown sugar and 1 sliced orange (unpeeled). Simmer for 30 minutes, strain, and serve hot or warm.

ROYALTY

Create a king, queen, prince, or princess costume by using any or all of the following:

Make a medium- or full-length EASY-SEW TUNIC (page 105) out of white or off-white fabric. Trim the neckline and bottom edge of tunic with a wide strip of shiny purple or gold fabric. Blanket trim is easiest to work with, although any shiny fabric remnants will do. Use more of this shiny fabric to make a sash belt and wristbands. Child wears tunic over white turtleneck and either tights or pants.

Child may prefer to wear a long QUICKIE VEST (page 106) over play or dress clothes. Trim all outside edges of vest with wide strips of shiny fabric, as shown. Use more shiny fabric and Velcro to make three or four tabs to close vest in front.

Make a CAPE (pages 111–14) out of the same shiny fabric used for tunic trim. (Or use a different color for cape: shiny purple, red, or gold are particularly royal.) Trim the cape with the white fabric used for the tunic. Stitch a 2-inch strip of fabric to cape's bottom edge. Stitch a wide collar to cape neckline, as shown.

For an extra-luxurious look, trim the cape with white fake fur instead of the tunic fabric. Decorate the fur with black permanent marker dots.

If desired, child can design and create a personal COAT OF ARMS from paper, felt, or aluminum foil. (See PAPER BAG KNIGHT, page 43, for ideas.) Stitch, tape, or glue coat of arms to front of tunic.

Child completes the royal look with a CROWN (page 126–27) and a MEDALLION (page 134).

Activity to try:

- Being treated like royalty seems to come naturally to children. Create a simple throne for your king or queen by covering a chair with a blanket, bedspread, or bath towel. Address the royal person as "Your Highness" or "Your Majesty," bow graciously, and allow your child to order you around . . . for about two minutes.

SUPERHEROES

Choose from the following costume ideas to create your child's favorite superhero.

SHINY HERO

Brightly colored, shiny vinyl cloth is available in fabric stores in different weights and with various backings. It's great for super-hero costumes because it is easily decorated with colorful plastic tape or self-adhesive vinyl paper, available in hardware stores.

Use light- or medium-weight vinyl cloth to make a No-Sew Tunic (page 103). Secure tunic with contrasting color vinyl cloth belt. Sides can also be held in place with plastic tape. Decorate costume with plastic tape trim and emblems cut from self-adhesive vinyl paper. (See EMBLEM TEMPLATES, page 135.)

Child wears costume over a sweatsuit, or leotard and tights. If possible, clothing should match tunic or trim color.

Gloves can be either winter gloves or inexpensive latex kitchen gloves. (See GLOVES, PAWS, AND CLAWS, page 145.)

LONG JOHN HERO

Inexpensive long underwear is perfect for creating a superhero costume. Choose white, gray, blue, navy, or red, and buy it over-size so the costume will last awhile.

Design your own emblem or copy your child's favorite hero's. Cut two emblems out of felt, and stitch or glue one to the front of the long underwear top. Stitch the second emblem to the back of a CAPE (pages 111–14).

If desired, add trim details directly to fabric with permanent marker. (A spiderweb pattern, for instance, works well.) Slide a paper grocery bag inside long underwear to prevent marker from leaking through.

Another way to decorate costume is to wrap colorful plastic tape loosely around legs and arms.

Child wears contrasting color shorts over the long john bottoms and contrasting color kneesocks for boots. Make a belt out of felt, fabric, vinyl cloth, or aluminum foil. Child wears a FABRIC EYE MASK (page 123), a purchased eye mask, or a HOOD (page 128).

SWEATSUIT HERO

Make a SWEATSHIRT CAPE (page 114), and attach emblems to sweatshirt front and cape back. Accessorize with belt, gloves, mask, and boots.

- For outdoor play, consider rain boots trimmed with plastic tape.

- If Superhero carries a weapon, refer to WEAPONS section, page 153.

Activities to try:

- Help your child create his or her own superhero, and design an original costume and emblem. Decide on the superhero's powers, weaknesses, friends, and foes.

- Make SUPERHERO TRADING CARDS. Cut paper rectangles $2\frac{1}{2} \times 3\frac{1}{2}$ inches. Use pencils and markers to draw your own versions of superheroes or villains on one side of each card. List important personal information—height, weight, secret identity, special powers, power ratings, personal history, and so on on the back of each card.

  To protect finished cards, cover both sides with clear, self-adhesive vinyl paper.

VAMPIRE

Child wears shiny, black CAPE with scalloped edge (page 113), black pants, white shirt, and white gloves. Make a gold MEDALLION (page 134) on a red ribbon. Use mousse or gel to slick back hair, and add an eyebrow pencil hairline to child's forehead, as shown. Complete the look with white face makeup and store-bought fangs.

PROPS, ACCESSORIES, AND MAKEUP

Props, accessories, and makeup are often the most important items in a costume. Many children choose a favorite prop first, and then think up and build a costume around it. Props are fun to make and can be used over and over again for all sorts of play.

The following supplies will get you started toward some great-looking results: corrugated cardboard, colored plastic tape, duct tape, colored cloth tape, glue, glitter, wire hangers, paper towel tubes, paper plates, markers, paints, spray paint (silver or gold), face makeup, eyebrow pencil, lipstick, corks, hair mousse or gel. A hot glue gun, although not a necessity, makes prop making even easier.

MASKS

HOW TO KEEP A MASK ON YOUR CHILD'S HEAD

Avoid that annoying "slip-down" problem by using string and heavy tape to make any mask more secure. Turn your mask (homemade or purchased) facedown. Tape one end of a 10-inch piece of string to the top of the mask. Then tape an 18-inch piece of string to one side of the mask, near an eyehole.

With child wearing mask, bring the 18-inch piece of string behind child's head and tape to other side of mask, next to eyehole. The mask should be comfortably snug.

While child holds mask in place, bring the 10-inch string over top of child's head and tie the loose end to the longer piece of string, as shown.

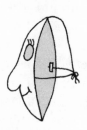

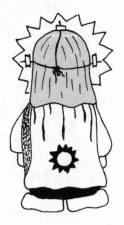

back view

PAPER PLATE MASKS

Make super fast and simple masks from plain, white paper plates. Cut eyeholes, then have child decorate bottom of plate with crayons or markers. If desired, holes can be cut for nose and mouth. Outside edge of plate can be trimmed with ears, fringe, and so on (see opposite).

For finishing details, see HOW TO KEEP A MASK ON YOUR CHILD'S HEAD, above.

kitty   lion   robot

FABRIC EYE MASK

Use two weights of fabric for these scarf-type masks. Stiff fabrics such as heavyweight felt, heavy knits, or sponge- or polyester-backed vinyl cloth are best for the front of the mask. Cut out the desired mask shape, and use chalk to gently mark eyehole location. (1) Cut almond-shaped eyeholes, starting small and enlarging as necessary. (2)

Use same-color lighter-weight fabric for sash ties. Stitch to sides of mask, as shown in Figure 3.

This mask is perfect for Zorro or WARRIOR TURTLE costumes.

★ *Note:* You might want to invest in a small, stiff-paper eye mask, available at toy stores. These masks are inexpensive and add a nice finishing touch to many costumes. Black is an especially useful color.

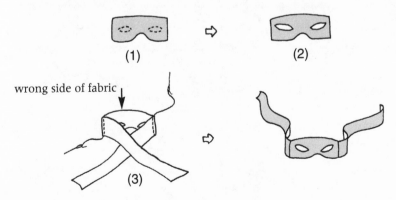

wrong side of fabric

(1)   (2)   (3)

HEADWEAR

PAPER PLATE HATS

Make a quick and silly hat from a paper or disposable plastic plate. Use 9-inch plates for little heads, 10-inch plates for older children. Start with the simple example in Figure 1. Cut along the dotted lines, remove the shaded area, and bend up the remaining "ears." (2) Wear the hat so that the plate is curving down.

Try cutting other designs for different results. (3)

Decorate with markers, crayons, pipe cleaners, paper scraps, and other items.

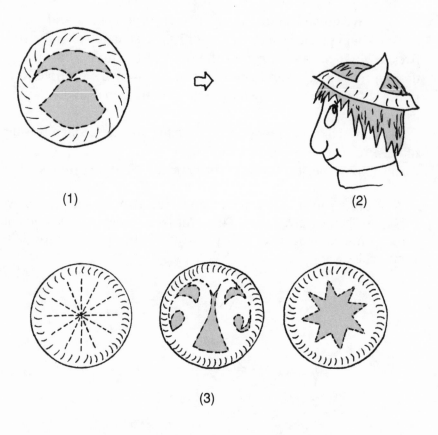

(1)   (2)

(3)

CONE HAT

Use a brown paper grocery bag, a large piece of white paper, or poster board to make a cone-shaped hat. Cut out a half circle with a radius of about 8 inches. (1) Cut off a 4-inch-wide pie-shaped section at one end. (2) Decorate the paper as desired (polka dots for a clown, stars and moons for a sorcerer, etc.). Reinforce the rounded edge with masking or strapping tape. (3) Form paper into a cone shape, and tape securely. (4) Thread yarn through masking tape on either side of hat to make ties. (5)

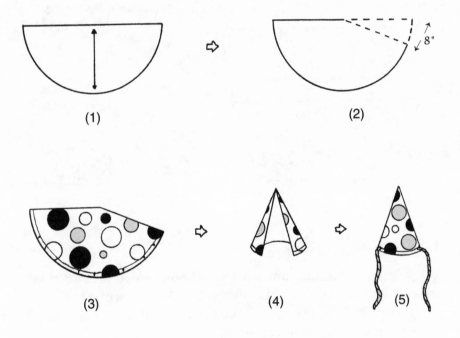

(1)   (2)

(3)   (4)   (5)

PAPER CROWNS

You can use almost any type of paper to make a crown, but fairly stiff paper is best, and the resulting crown will last longer. Measure around your child's head to find the length you'll need. Cut the paper strip a bit longer and 3–4 inches high.

Decide on a crown design (see examples), and then draw and cut out your crown. Decorate crown with markers, paint, crayons, glitter, or jewels made of paper or foil. Tape securely to fit.

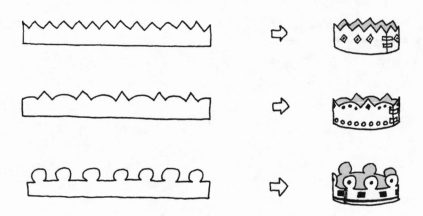

FOIL CROWN

Use a length of aluminum foil long enough to go around child's head. Fold the foil, shiny side out, into a 3-inch strip. On the side of the strip with loose edges of foil, run a line of strapping or masking tape, about 1½ inches from the top. (1)

Use sharp scissors to cut triangles along the top edge, as shown. (2) The scissor cuts will seal the layers of foil together, and the line of tape will prevent the foil from tearing.

Decorate the crown with paper jewels, and tape together to fit child. If desired, pointy tips of crown can be bent slightly outward. (3)

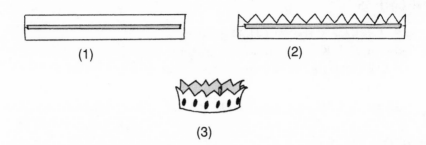

(1)

(2)

(3)

PIPE CLEANER CROWNS

Craft stores sell a wide selection of extralong (12-inch), heavy-weight pipe cleaners in an array of colors. Sparkly silver or gold pipe cleaners make an especially nice-looking, delicate crown.

The examples pictured below use between four and ten pipe cleaners per crown. To construct a simple crown, start with a circle that fits your child's head, and attach additional pipe cleaners to create the look you want. You might also try weaving the pipe cleaners, using contrasting colors, or twisting the pipe cleaners to make different shapes.

★ *Note:* Pipe cleaners can also be used to make matching bracelets and rings.

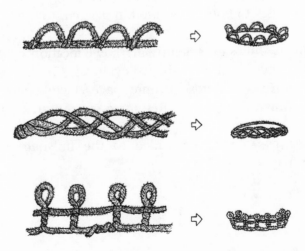

HELMETS

HOODS

Use stiff, nonfraying fabrics to make a variety of hood styles. Heavyweight felt comes in lots of bright colors. Or look for various types and weights of vinyl cloth backed with sponge, a soft polyester material, or a polyester bonding.

Some hoods cover part or all of the child's face; others leave face exposed and ready for makeup or a mask. All hoods consist of two identical side panels and a long, 3–4-inch-wide strip down the center. Use the patterns in Figures 1, 2, and 3 as a general guide.

Measure the side of your child's head to determine the length and width of side panels. Length is from very top of child's head to shoulder level, minus 1–2 inches. Width is from behind ear to cheekbone, plus 3–4 inches.

Measure from base of child's neck, over child's head, and onto face (forehead, nose level, or below chin) to determine length of center strip.

Cut fabric and stitch as shown. (4) Turn hood right side out.

Stitch ribbon ties to bottom of hood, if desired, to hold hood in place. (1)

If hood covers child's eyes, gently mark eye location with chalk, remove hood, and cut almond-shaped eyeholes. (2)

If hood is for Ninja Warrior costume (page 9), cut a narrow oval for eyes, as shown in Figure 3. Reinforce cut-out area with top-stitching.

Ears or Antennae may be added to the finished hood, as described on pages 142–44.

HOODS

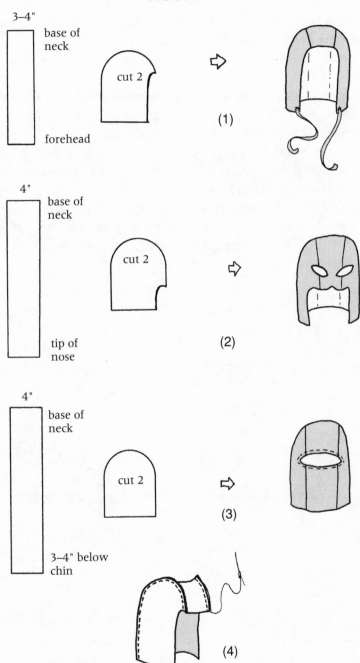

3–4"

base of
neck

cut 2

forehead

(1)

4"

base of
neck

cut 2

tip of
nose

(2)

4"

base of
neck

cut 2

3–4" below
chin

(3)

(4)

ADVENTURER'S HAT

Choose a fairly stiff fabric (felt is perfect), or sandwich a piece of interfacing between two layers of fabric.

Cut out four of the shape shown in Figure 1. If necessary, adjust size to fit child.

Place two fabric pieces with right sides together, and sew straight bottom edge. (2) Turn right side out and iron. Topstitch folded edge, if desired. (3) Repeat steps 2 and 3 for the other two fabric pieces.

Place the two double-layer pieces together, and sew the curved edge, stitching through all four fabric layers. (4) Trim the curved seam to about ¼ inch. (5)

Turn bottom edge up, and tack in place with a few stitches. (6)

Make a brightly colored feather from a double layer of felt or paper, or use a real feather. Attach with a few stitches. (7)

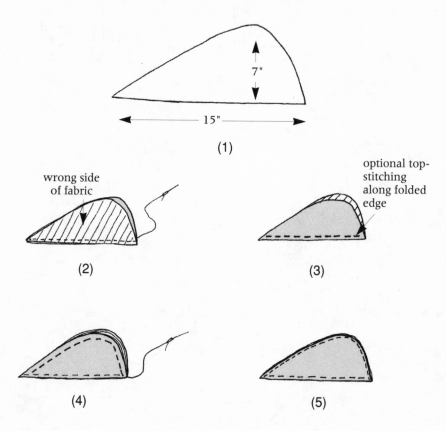

7"

15"

(1)

wrong side
of fabric

(2)

optional top-
stitching
along folded
edge

(3)

(4)

(5)

(6)   (7)

TRIANGLE KERCHIEF

Fold a square bandana or scarf on the diagonal. Place on child's head, and tie ends at back of neck. Child can wear kerchief behind ears, secured with bobby pins, for HIPPIE costume. Or kerchief can cover one or both ears, for PIRATE, GYPSY, or FORTUNE TELLER costume. This looks especially convincing when worn with PIRATE OR GYPSY EARRING (page 134).

JEWELRY AND ACCESSORIES

FOIL JEWELRY

Make shiny silver ropes from lengths of loosely rolled and twisted aluminum foil. Use these ropes to make a quick necklace, bracelet, or headband. Wrap foil ropes with colorful pipe cleaners for an interesting effect.

FOIL BEAD NECKLACE

Tear aluminum foil into many pieces, each about 1½ inches square. Loosely crumple each square into a ball, about ⅜ inch in diameter. Do *not* compact the foil, or the needle won't poke through.

Using a heavy needle and thread, thread foil balls to make a necklace.

FOIL BELT AND WRISTBANDS

Use a length of aluminum foil long enough to go around child's waist. Fold the foil, shiny side out, until it is a strip about 1½–2 inches wide. For extra durability, run a strip of masking or strapping tape along the inside. Decorate the belt, if desired, and tape around child.

Use shorter lengths of foil to make wristbands.

HALO

Use a length of aluminum foil long enough to go around child's head, overlapping 2–3 inches. Fold the foil, shiny side out, until it is a strip about 1 inch wide. Tape securely to form a headband. (1)

Measure a length of foil about 17 inches long, and cut in half lengthwise so you have two pieces, each 6 inches wide. Fold one piece into a thin strip, ¼ inch wide. Wrap this strip around a large cylinder (a large oatmeal box is just right) to make a perfect circle. Tape in place with clear tape to form the halo. (2)

Cut the second piece of foil into a strip, 3 × 12 inches. Use this piece to cover a plastic drinking straw, shiny side out. (3) Attach the foil-covered straw to the headband and halo by bending the extra foil at the ends of the straw and securing with clear tape. (4) Be sure to attach the straw to the headband and halo where the foil overlaps and has been taped.

See also FOIL CROWN, page 126.

HALO

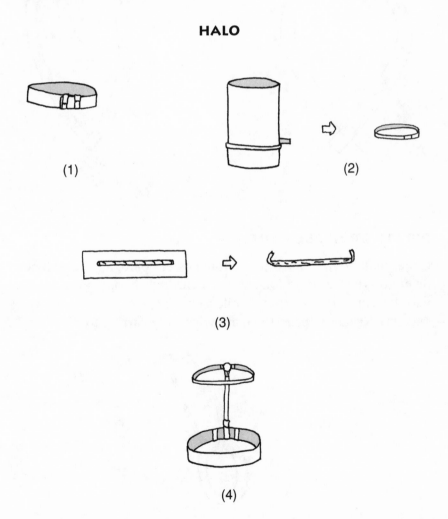

(1)

(2)

(3)

(4)

MEDALLION

Cut a medallion shape out of poster board or cardboard. Either cover it with aluminum foil or paint it gold or silver.

Sew a length of 1-inch wide ribbon as shown below, so that it fits easily over child's head. Trim edges, and attach medallion to ribbon with heavy needle and thread.

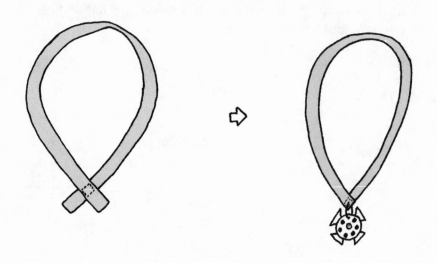

PIRATE OR GYPSY EARRING

Cut a small hoop shape out of white poster board, and color it gold or bright yellow. Tie a loop of yarn through hoop, and adjust so yarn fits comfortably around child's entire ear. Cover that ear with TRIANGLE KERCHIEF (page 131), allowing only earring to show.

EMBLEM TEMPLATES

Borrow emblem ideas from real life, comic books, or television, or make up your own. A bright, eye-catching insignia spices up a costume and gives your child's character a special identity.

Draw a paper pattern of the desired symbol (superhero, lightning bolt, royal crest, police officer, etc.). Decide on the colors, and cut the design out of felt. Glue or stitch the pieces together (fabric glue is great for gluing felt to felt), and attach to long john top, sweatshirt, tunic, or cape.

WANDS

FAIRY WAND

Sketch a circle, emblem, or the star shape shown in Figure 1 (opposite) onto cardboard or poster board, and cut it out. If using poster board, you may want to cut out two shapes to glue together for extra thickness and durability. Be sure to include the tab on the bottom of the shape, to attach it to the wand handle.

Wand handle can be a purchased wooden dowel, a cardboard tube from a wire clothes hanger, a chopstick, a wooden spoon, or any similar object. Use heavy tape to secure the cardboard shape to the handle. (2) If using a cardboard wire hanger tube, slit one end, and slide the tab into the slit. Then wrap with tape to secure. (3)

Cover the handle with aluminum foil and clear tape, white plastic tape, or paint. Decorate the star or other shape with aluminum foil, paint, or glitter.

MAGICIAN'S WAND

The cardboard tube from a wire clothes hanger is perfect for a magician's wand. Cut off a piece of tubing about 8 inches long. Cover it with black plastic tape or cloth tape (available in hardware stores). Wrap each end with white plastic tape or white paper.

FAIRY WAND

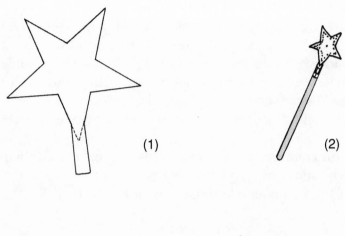

(1)

(2)

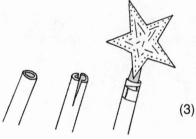

(3)

HAIR

YARN WIG

Find a table or other surface that is about 30–36 inches wide. Loosely wrap yarn at least 50–60 times around the table. (1) Carefully remove yarn from around table, and lay the center of the yarn over a 2 × 6–inch strip of felt or other fabric, as shown. (2)

Cover yarn with a second strip of fabric. Pull a few strands of yarn forward at each end, for bangs in the front and to cover the back of child's head. (3)

Stitch through all layers of fabric and yarn, by machine or by hand. (4)

Set wig on child's head to decide on length of hair and bangs. Remove wig, and trim yarn with scissors. (4)

Child wears wig under a knit hat, cap, or kerchief.

Variations:

- Make a wig using *jute twine* instead of yarn. When the wig is complete, unravel the strands of twine for an especially bushy look.

- Wigs may be braided or tied in pigtails.

YARN WIG

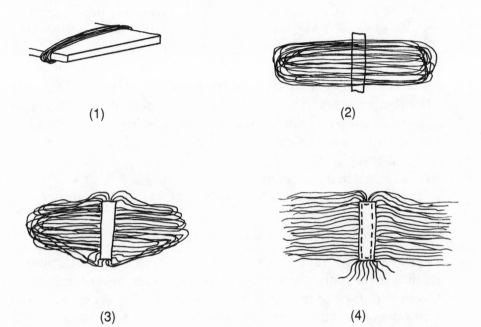

(1)

(2)

(3)

(4)

BRAIDS

Use three pairs of old panty hose to make these easy braids. Overlap tops of panty hose, and secure with safety pins, as shown in Figure 1 (opposite), or use a basting stitch (Figure 2).

Loosely braid three legs together on each side, securing bottoms of braids with rubber bands, elastics, or colorful ribbons. (2)

Use sharp scissors to cut a hole, 3–4 inches in diameter, through all layers of the panty hose tops. (3) Braids now fit as a "headband" around child's head. If desired, wrap area around hole with yarn for a neater look. (4)

Tuck child's hair and panty hose tops under a hat or kerchief, and adjust braids so that they are behind child's ears. (5)

GEORGE WASHINGTON WIG

An old swim cap is the base of this wig. Staple a 6 × 1–inch piece of fabric to the bottom of the cap in the back. Use rubber cement to cover the outside of the cap with cotton balls. Glue cotton balls to both sides of the fabric strip to form a "ponytail." Allow to dry.

Have child try on wig, and add cotton balls to cover "bald spots."

Tie a black ribbon around ponytail, 1 inch from end, to form a bow.

BRAIDS

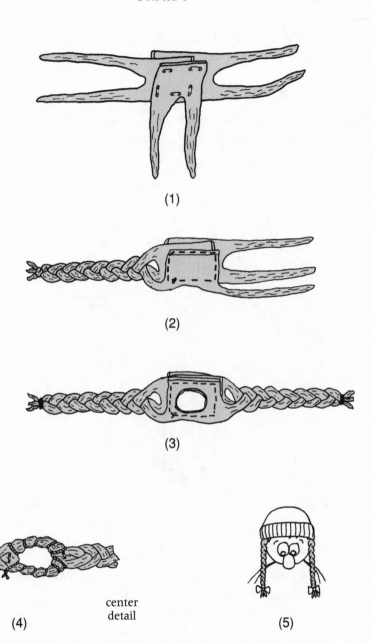

(1)

(2)

(3)

(4)

center
detail

(5)

EARS AND ANTENNAE

Paper or fabric ears attach easily to a knit hat, plastic headband, or HOOD (page 128). Once again, felt is the recommended fabric.

FLOPPY EARS

These ears work best attached to a hood or knit hat. Cut out the ear shape you want, and stitch or safety-pin bottom of ears to fabric, as shown below.

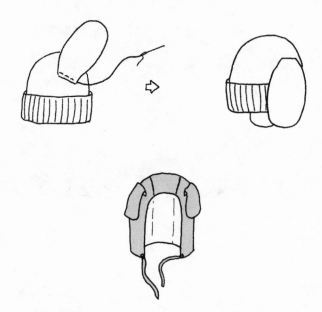

PERKY EARS

Using fairly stiff fabric, cut out the ear shape you want, baste as shown at the top of page 143 (1), and gather the bottom edge. (2) Attach ears to knit hat or hood with a few stitches, or secure to plastic headband with tape. (3)

PERKY EARS

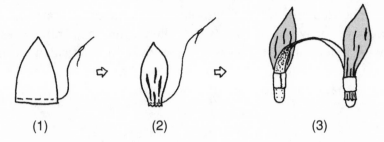

(1)   (2)   (3)

BENDABLE EARS

Cut four ears and stitch together, as shown below, to form two double-thickness ears. (1)

Bend pipe cleaners and slide inside ears. Adjust so that pipe cleaners are next to outer edges. If you are using felt, the texture of the fabric will hold the pipe cleaners in place. (2)

Attach ears to hat, hood, or headband, and bend in desired position. (3)

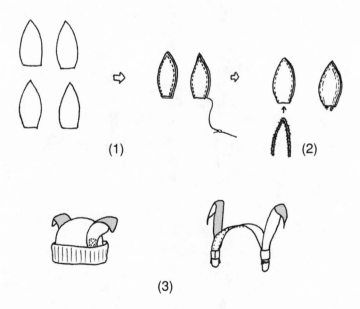

(1)   (2)

(3)

ANTENNAE

Use pipe cleaners to create simple insect antennae, sparkling fairy antennae, or wild and crazy space alien antennae. Craft stores sell a wide selection of extra-long, heavyweight pipe cleaners in an array of colors. Stitch the antennae to a knit hat or a HOOD (page 128), or tape them to a plastic headband.

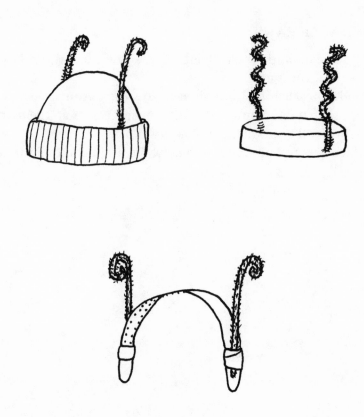

GLOVES, PAWS, AND CLAWS

Put the finishing touches on any costume with flashy handwear. Look for inexpensive latex dishwashing gloves in grocery stores. These usually come in bright yellow or orange. You can trim the cuffs or fingertips with scissors, draw details on them with permanent marker, or add strips of colored plastic tape. (1)

Winter gloves or mittens can be modified for many costumes. Animal claws can be slivers of white tape or felt triangles glued or stitched to fingertips. (2) Decorate mittens with felt shapes that have been glued or stitched on. (3)

Oversize, heavy gloves can be worn as part of a MONSTER, ROBOT, or ASTRONAUT costume.

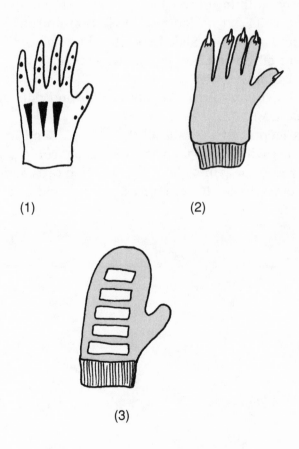

(1)   (2)

(3)

EXTRA ARM

To make this funny special effect, you will need two *identical* long-sleeved shirts (turtlenecks or long-sleeved T-shirts are perfect), a loose-fitting shirt that buttons up the front, and three *identical* gloves or mittens.

Pull a wire hanger into a long, thin shape, as shown. (1) Use pliers to bend the handle over. Cover any sharp ends with duct tape, and tape the hanger together, if necessary. (2)

Roll hanger inside a hand towel or lightweight bath towel. Secure with rubber bands. (3)

Child puts on first turtleneck. Push towel-wrapped hanger through right arm of second turtleneck. Child puts on second turtleneck, fitting only *left* arm through sleeve.

Help child put on loose-fitting button-up shirt. Slide child's *left* arm into left sleeve. Slide Extra Arm into right sleeve. Button front of shirt at top and bottom, allowing child's *right* arm to stick out front of shirt.

Roll up outer shirtsleeves above elbow on child's left arm and on Extra Arm.

Put identical gloves on all three arms. Bend Extra Arm into a natural position, and tape an empty paper cup, a pencil, or another lightweight prop into glove. Child should carry some other prop in one other hand. If desired, the extra hand can rest in a pants pocket.

EXTRA ARM

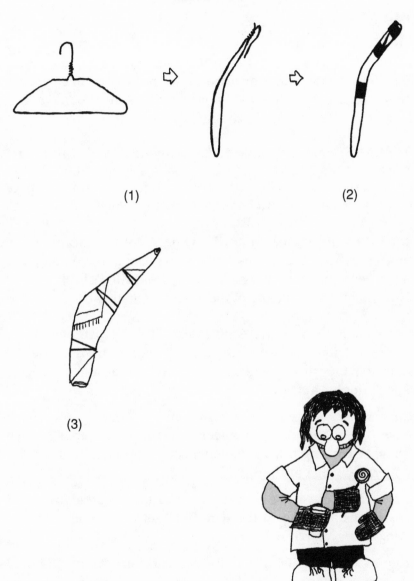

(1)

(2)

(3)

WINGS

WIRE WINGS

Gently squash the hooked handles of two wire coat hangers, and fasten them together with duct tape, as shown. (1 and 2 opposite)

Tie a long ribbon, scarf, or old necktie around the taped area to serve as a harness to hold the wings on. The scarf should be long enough to go around child's chest. (3)

✱ *Note:* You may want to add a second ribbon or scarf to prevent wings from sliding down child's back. Figure 6 shows wings with two ribbons attached. WIRE-WING ANGEL illustration (page 107) demonstrates how ribbons are tied across child's chest.

Bend the wire hangers into the wing shape you want. Some examples are shown in Figure 4. For some costumes, you may also want to bend the wings back a bit, away from child's back.

Cover the wings with any of the following materials:

- *White or colored panty hose.* Cut the legs off an old pair of white or colored panty hose, and stretch a leg over each wing. Tie the ends together in the center, as shown. (5) Decorate with glue and glitter for ANGEL or FAIRY.

- *Plastic bubble wrap.* Use a hot glue gun or clear tape to attach sheets of bubble packing material to the wire frame of each wing. Leave long strips of material hanging from outer edges for a more flowing effect. (6)

- *Tissue paper.* Use a hot glue gun or clear tape to attach white or colored tissue paper to the wire frame of each wing. Decorate wings with colored markers.

- *Fabric.* Cover each wing with lightweight, gauzy fabric. Recycled curtains are perfect, or look for chiffon, decorative lace, or tulle in your fabric store. Either hand sew or hot glue the fabric in place. If desired, leave long strips of fabric hanging from outer wing edges, as in Figure 6.

WIRE WINGS

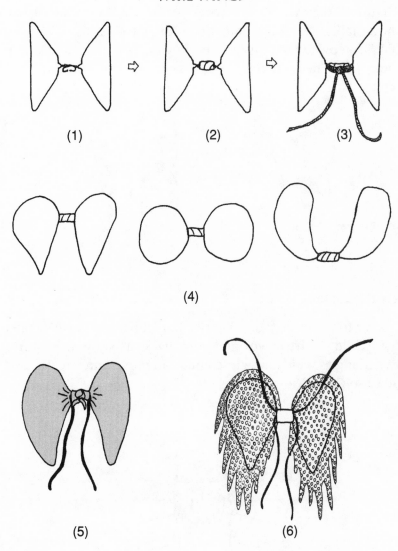

(1) (2) (3)

(4)

(5) (6)

- For BUTTERFLY wings, bind *two* sets of wings together, as shown in Figure 7 (below). Cover wings with white or colored panty hose, fabric, or tissue paper. Sew or hot glue brightly colored fabric pieces to the outside of each wing. (8) Attach a second ribbon, if needed, to hold wings securely and comfortably on child's back.

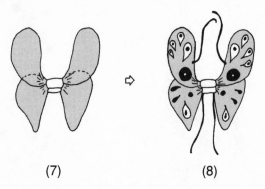

(7)   (8)

FABRIC WINGS

Cut *large* triangles of gauzy, lightweight fabric, and baste or safety-pin to child's shirtsleeves and shirt back, as shown. Be sure to make triangles wide enough so child can move arms freely.

See also CIRCLE COSTUME, page 99.

TAILS

BUNNY TAIL

Make a pom-pom tail by loosely wrapping yarn (the color of the bunny) around a 5-inch piece of cardboard about 100–150 times. (1)

Slide roll of yarn off cardboard, and use a long piece of yarn or heavyweight thread to tie the roll tightly in the middle. (2)

Cut all the loops of yarn, and trim to form a ball shape. (3) Do *not* cut the two long pieces of yarn or thread.

Thread a needle through the long yarn or thread ends, and sew the tail to the child's costume.

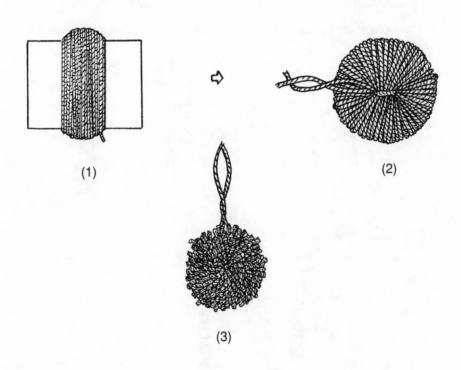

(1)

(2)

(3)

YARN TAIL

Find a chair back or other object that is 15–20 inches across. Wrap yarn about 30 times around the chair back. (1)

Use a separate piece of yarn or heavyweight thread to tie the yarn together. (2)

Remove yarn from chair back, and tie a separate piece of yarn around "tail," about 1–2 inches from the top. (3)

Cut bottom loops, and trim tail to desired length. (3)

Variations:

• Braid part or all of tail. Secure end with a ribbon. (4)

• Tie tail with thin ribbon every 3–4 inches. (5)

• Use *jute twine* instead of yarn, unraveling strands for an extra-bushy look.

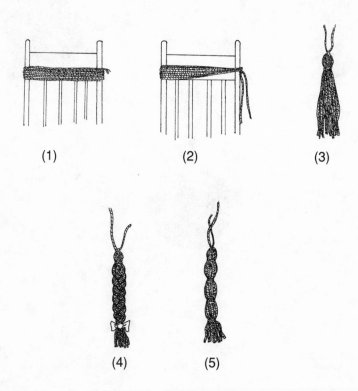

(1)   (2)   (3)

(4)   (5)

FABRIC TAIL

Make this simple tail by sewing a long tube of fabric, as shown. Use a chopstick or dowel to turn the fabric right side out. Decorate tail, if desired, stuff loosely with polyester filling or old panty hose, and stitch or safety-pin in place.

For a tail with personality, consider sliding two or three heavy-weight pipe cleaners inside the fabric tube, toward the end. Stuff tail loosely, attach to costume, then bend or curl.

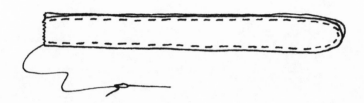

WEAPONS

A WORD ABOUT WEAPONS

Some children show no interest in weapons; others become obsessed with them. Some parents and caregivers are comfortable with toy weaponry; others are not.

If your child's fascination with weapons exceeds your own, homemade weapons may be a good compromise. While working creatively with your child, you can outline some rules about weapon use in your home. Your finished product will be satisfying for your child, won't hurt anyone or make noise, and will eventually fall apart!

Another form of compromise might be a squirt gun or similar inexpensive plastic weapon.

SPEAR

Cut a piece of corrugated cardboard, about 3½ inches wide and 24 or more inches long. Use a razor knife to score the cardboard, as shown in Figure 1. (*Scoring* means cutting through just the top layer of cardboard. Do *not* cut all the way through!)

Cut two identical spear points out of cardboard. (2)

Fold the long cardboard piece along scored lines, as shown. (3)

Slide the spear points inside the folded cardboard. (4)

Tightly wrap spear handle with brown or black cloth tape. Cover spear points with silver duct tape. (5)

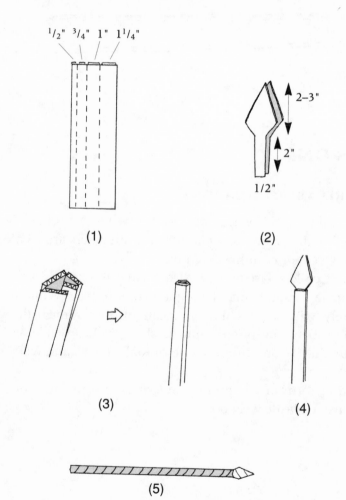

BOW AND ARROWS

Make a bow from a thin, flexible stick about 2–3 feet long. Use a knife to cut notches in each end of the stick, and stretch a string from end to end.

Plastic drinking straws make safe, lightweight arrows. Make feathers and arrow points from stiff paper (paper plates are a good weight), coloring them with marker or crayon. Cut slits in the straws, and attach the feathers and points with clear tape, as shown.

Activity to try:

• Make an arrow QUIVER. Flatten one end of a paper towel tube, and tape it closed. (1) Cover the tube with brown paper or brown cloth tape. Stuff the bottom of the tube with a couple of paper towels, so that arrows will stick out the top. Attach a loop of thin ribbon or heavy cord at top and bottom of quiver. (2)

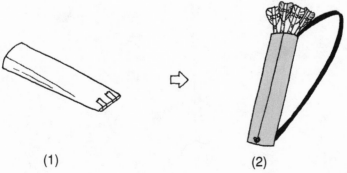

(1)   (2)

Props, Accessories, and Makeup **155**

DAGGERS AND SWORDS

Make a sturdy, long-lasting sword or dagger out of corrugated cardboard, black or brown cloth tape, and silver duct tape. First, decide on the sword or dagger design. Some examples are illustrated in Figure 5 (below). You may want to sketch a pattern on paper before cutting the cardboard.

Cut *four* thicknesses of blades and cross guards (quillons). (1)

Put the four blades together, and secure with a piece of tape. (2)

Put two cross guard pieces on each side of the blade, and secure with black or brown cloth tape. (3) Cover the entire handle with black or brown tape. (4)

Wrap the blade with silver duct tape. (4)

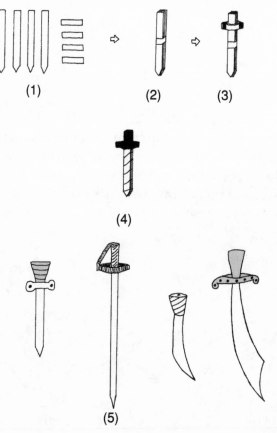

(1)   (2)   (3)

(4)

(5)

Activities to try:

- If desired, make a SHEATH for your sword or dagger. Use cardboard at least 2 inches longer than the sword's blade. Fold the cardboard into a flattened tube slightly wider than the sword, and cover with cloth tape or duct tape. (1) To attach it to a belt, cut the front of the sheath as shown in Figure 2.

  Cut a 7-inch length of cloth tape or duct tape, and line the sticky side with a 4-inch length of tape. (3) Attach the ends of this lined piece of tape to the sheath top, as shown, to form a belt loop. (4)

- Some superheroes carry swords down their backs. A more comfortable alternative is to make an arrow QUIVER (page 155), flattened slightly to fit the sword.

SHEATH

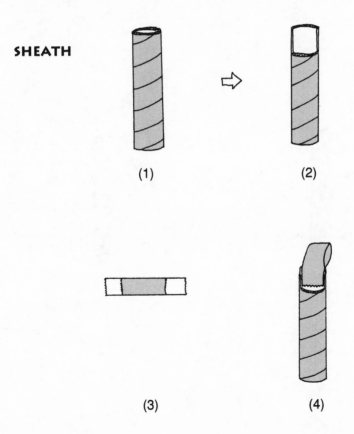

(1)   (2)

(3)   (4)

AXE

Cut the shape illustrated in Figure 1 (below) from a cardboard box. Fold in half, as shown. (2) Attach to a paper towel tube (or a short dowel) using silver duct tape. (3) Wrap the entire "blade" with duct tape. Wrap the handle with brown cloth tape (found in hardware stores) or masking tape. (4)

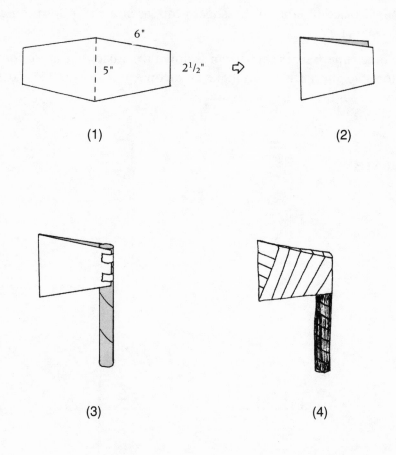

(1)

(2)

(3)

(4)

SHIELDS

Shields come in all sorts of shapes, colors, and sizes. Look at the drawings on page 160 or those for the PAPER BAG KNIGHT costume (page 43), or make a trip to the library for a book about armor and weaponry. Your child may want to sketch the shape and design of the shield on paper.

For a simple, flat shield, cut two shield shapes out of corrugated cardboard. (1) Cut slits in one shield piece, as shown in Figure 2. Cut two strips of cardboard, 1 × 16 inches, and cover both sides with duct tape or colored cloth tape. Slide these strips into the slits, adjusting the length for handles, and trimming if necessary. (3) Turn shield piece over, and secure the strip ends with glue and strong tape. (4)

Glue the second shield piece over the strip ends. Allow glue to dry, then cover shield with paint, silver duct tape, or colored cloth tape. Some DECORATION SUGGESTIONS are listed on page 160.

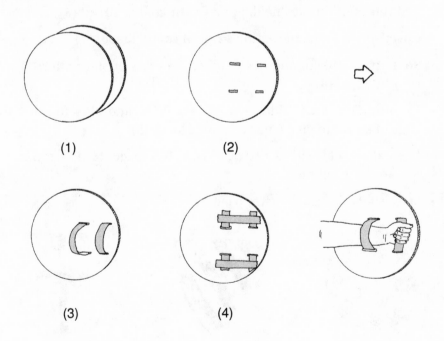

(1)   (2)

(3)   (4)

If a bent shield is desired, cut out two shield shapes, and lightly score the areas to be bent. (5) Follow directions for handle strips, and glue pieces together.

★ *Note:* Scoring means cutting through just the top layer of cardboard. Do *not* cut all the way through!

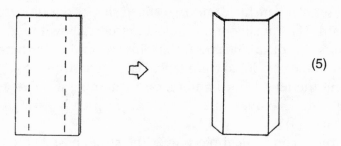

(5)

Decoration suggestions:

- Glue individual cups from cardboard egg cartons to outer edge and center of round shield. Spray-paint gold or silver. (6)

- Cover shield with alternating strips of colored tape. (7)

- Spray-paint shield, and decorate with a cross or star pattern in colorful tape. (8)

- Cut a long, 2-inch wide strip of cardboard, and glue to outer edge of shield to give a more convex look. (8)

- Decorate shield with a COAT OF ARMS. See page 43, PAPER BAG KNIGHT, for examples.

- See also PAPER PLATE SHIELD, page 44.

(6)   (7)   (8)

NINJA WEAPONS

Nunchaku

You will need two toilet paper tubes, string or yarn, newspaper, and black cloth tape to make this basic ninja weapon.

Measure three 24-inch lengths of string or black yarn, and loosely braid them together. Knot each end to keep the braid from coming undone.

Lay two full sheets of newspaper together, and fold, as shown below, to get a $4\frac{1}{2} \times 22$–inch strip. (1) Lay one end of the braided string across one end of the strip, with the knot hanging out, (2) and roll into a tight roll.

Slide newspaper roll inside one of the toilet paper tubes. (3)

Repeat steps 1, 2, and 3 for second toilet paper tube.

Wrap tubes with black cloth tape, covering ends first and then sides.

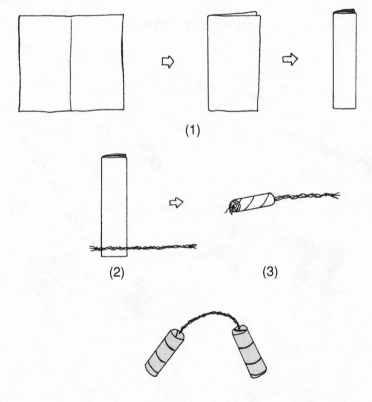

Shuriken (Throwing stars)

Child can carry a selection of these stars in a pocket, pouch, or waist pack. Cut the shapes out of cardboard, using the examples as guides. The stars are about 2 inches across. Children can design their own. Paint or color both sides of the stars black or gold.

Bo or Hanbo (Wooden staff)

A *bo* is 6 feet long; a *hanbo* is 3 feet long. Follow directions for SPEAR (page 154), omitting the spear point. Cover the staff with either black or brown cloth tape.

Ninja Sword

Follow directions for DAGGERS AND SWORDS (page 156) to make a medium-length, straight sword in a black sheath. Ninjas tuck this sword into a sash belt.

NINJA WEAPONS

RAY GUNS

A stylized, homemade "ray gun" is a more creative project, and might result in less violent play than a regular gun. Rather than hurt, a ray gun's blast can temporarily immobilize a victim, or cause hysterical laughter, instant sleep, slow-motion movements, and so on.

Cut four thicknesses of the gun design out of corrugated cardboard. Put the shapes together, and wrap with silver duct tape or colorful cloth tape. If desired, decorate with brightly colored plastic tape, as shown below.

★ *Note:* Other props featured with specific costumes include:
Box Walkie-Talkies, page 18
Paper Cup Walkie-Talkies, pages 18–19
Ice Axe, page 23
Megaphone, pages 27–28

MAKEUP TIPS

Makeup is often a safe alternative to masks, which can slip around and hamper vision. A little makeup goes a long way and can be used for many different looks. Use small amounts on young children, and avoid putting makeup near eyes, so cleanup will be easy. Rubbing a little cold cream into skin *before* makeup is applied makes removal easier.

Here are some easy makeup suggestions:

Animal whiskers —

Use brown or black eyebrow pencil or eyeliner pen to darken tip of nose, and draw three or four whiskers on lower cheeks.

Stitches, scars, and gaping wounds —

Draw Frankenstein-like stitches with black eyebrow pencil. Wonderfully unpleasant wounds can be outlined in black pencil and filled in with red lipstick.

Burnt cork makeup —

Burn the end of a cork, and let cool for a minute. Apply to child's face for a convincing BEARD, mustache, or five o'clock shadow. Burnt cork is also perfect for adding DIRT to the faces, arms, and legs of cave dwellers, monsters, and other tough-looking characters.

Mousse or gel for hair —

Rock stars, vampires, monsters, cave dwellers, and others all can benefit from spiked or slicked down hair. Liberal amounts of mousse or gel make hair styling easy.

Lipstick and blush —

Even the tiniest addition of basic makeup can satisfy young fairies, royalty, angels, butterflies, and others.

INDEX